Hot Rodding
INTERNATIONAL

Contents

Introduction	2	Larry O'Toole
Roland Stockhausen 1932 Ford Roadster	4	Ascheberg, GERMANY
Gallery: Ian Guy	10	Automotive Artist - UK
Event: Pre '49 Street Rod Nationals	18	Taupo, NEW ZEALAND
Model Car History	26	Alan Barton showcases model cars though the ages
Old Car City USA	36	Where old cars go to die – Georgia, USA
Andy Saunders' 1937 Cord Custom	46	Poole, Dorset, UK
40th Anniversary Australian Street Rodding magazine	56	Castlemaine, Victoria, AUSTRALIA
Event: Castlemaine Pre-Nationals Rod Run	60	Castlemaine, Victoria, AUSTRALIA
Event: ASRF Street Rod Nationals	66	Bendigo, Victoria, AUSTRALIA
Jack Martin's 1930 Model A Ford Coupe	80	Auckland, NEW ZEALAND
Event: Tucson Dragway Reunion	86	Tucson, Arizona, USA
Event: NSRA Street Rod Nationals	92	Louisville, Kentucky, USA
Event: Rattle Trap – Beach Racing	102	Crowdy Head, NSW, AUSTRALIA
John Martin's 1934 Ford Hot Rod Coupe	110	Nixa, Missouri, USA
Event: Bonneville Speed Week – The Album	116	Wendover, Utah, USA
Event: Kumeu Car Festival	128	Auckland, NEW ZEALAND
Profile: Lenny Souter	138	Mansfield, Victoria, AUSTRALIA
Event: Top End Rumble, an Epic Rod Run to Darwin and Back	148	Darwin, Northern Territory, AUSTRALIA
Charlie's Pride: 1948 Ford Convertible & 1932 Ford Coupe	162	Farady, Victoria, AUSTRALIA
Event: European Street Rod Nats and UK Hot Rod Supernats	176	Old Warden, UK
Hot Rodders' Handy Hints	188	Clever Tricks from around the world of Hot Rodding
Event: The Boogaloo Invitational	198	Castlemaine, Victoria, AUSTRALIA

Front cover photo: The beautifully detailed 331 Chrysler Hemi engine in Roland Stockhausen's '32 Ford hiboy roadster from Germany (see feature starting on page 4).

Published in 2018 by Graffiti Publications Pty. Ltd.,
69 Forest Street, Castlemaine, 3450 Victoria, Australia
Phone International: 61 3 5472 3653 or 61 3 5472 3805
Email: info@graffitipub.com.au
www.graffitipub.com.au
Publisher/Editor: Larry O'Toole
Text & Production: Larry O'Toole, Al O'Toole, Mary-Anna Brennand
Sales & Marketing: Mary O'Toole, Wendy Thomas, Nicky West
Photos: Larry O'Toole, Al O'Toole, Mary O'Toole, Greg Stokes, Alan Barton, Matt Woods, John Martin, Mark Bieke, Ray Charlton, Show N Go Photography, Julie Loomes.

The information in this publication is true and complete to the best of our knowledge. All recommendations are made without any guarantee on the part of the author or publisher, who also disclaim any liability incurred in connection with the use of this data or specific details.

We recognise that some words, model names and designations mentioned herein, are the property of the trademark holder. We use them for identification purposes only. This is not an official publication.

Graffiti Publications titles are also available at discounts in bulk quantity for industrial or sales promotional use. For details contact Graffiti Publications Ph: (613) 5472 3653.
Printed & bound in Singapore by SC (Sang Choy) International Pte Ltd.
ISSN: 1836-2850.
ISBN: 9780949398215

Larry O'Toole

Introduction

In the world of automotive publishing I consider it quite an achievement that Hot Rodding International is now 10 years old. Few publishers would describe the past decade as prime time for printed publications but we have survived against the odds. Of course it is something of an advantage being an annual publication so we aren't caught up in the cycle of monthly deadlines that are the norm for most magazines like our companion publication Australian Street Rodding.

Technology is rapidly changing the world in countless ways, not just in publishing. I'm sure we will look back in the future and recognize what an exciting, unpredictable time we all experienced in this period.

Digital technology has rapidly changed every industry and hobby that it has touched and hot rodding is no exception. Look at how advanced aftermarket engine development has become thanks to the application of this digital technology that now allows us to take an old engine and make it as efficient as a brand new one. That's only one aspect of the application of digital technology in the hot rodding sphere. There are many others. Yet sitting in amongst all of this new technology we now have whole movements of hot rodders dedicated to keeping their style of street rod as anti-new technology as possible. Perfect!

We don't want everything about this hobby to become predictable and high tech, it prospers most when there is complete diversity, just as human life itself does. Imagine how boring it would be if every hot rod had a Chevy LS engine powering it. Sure they are efficient and powerful and ideal for many projects, but don't you just love to see an old flathead four or V8 dressed to kill and sitting in a hot rod engine bay for all to see and admire?

Rejoice in our many differences, throw yourself completely into your own particular street rod project and build it your way, not to suit someone else's interpretation. Then when it is done we can stand together at the next show or rod run and rattle on about the virtues of our particular choice in hobby vehicle until the Studebakers come home.

Let's keep things unpredictable!

Roland Stockhausen
Ascheberg, Germany

Building and owning a street rod in many of the European countries isn't always easy. Stringent regulations make it difficult at times to gain compliance, but despite that difficulty the hobby is gaining momentum. Germany is typical and it is where Roland Stockhausen has achieved his dream to own a Deuce hiboy roadster. Not just any Deuce hiboy roadster, nothing less than a Hemi powered, black painted thing of beauty that could hold its own in any street rod friendly country. Just how good Roland's '32 Ford is can be gauged by the fact that he was a Top Ten finalist at the European Street Rod Nationals held at Old Warden in England in August 2017.

Roland is no newcomer to the performance car hobby, he has been involved for over 40 years, starting out with chopper bikes, moving on to muscle cars with a '69 Pontiac GTO and following that with a 426 Hemi powered '67 Dodge Coronet. He has since spent eight years on the roadster project and the influence of that Hemi in the Coronet obviously had some bearing on the choice of powerplant for the roadster. This time it is a smaller Hemi, a 331 cubic inch version from a '55 Chrysler. But we are getting ahead of ourselves, let's roll back to an earlier stage of the project to learn how Roland achieved his dream.

Back in 2009 Roland laid down €30,000.00 for the basic package on which to base his hiboy project. For that outlay he took receipt of a rolling chassis, reproduction body plus a GM engine and went to work. There is no doubt Roland has captured the essence of a traditional style hiboy, yet he has managed to add his own personal touches that set it apart from most.

Much of the running gear is almost standard fare for a Deuce hiboy in that it uses a Super Bell drilled and dropped front axle held in place with a four bar system and directed by a Vega steering box set up in cross-steer fashion. Likewise the rear end is typical hiboy with four link equipped nine inch Ford third member that features a Detroit Locker centre and transverse spring rear suspension. The rear end uses the standard Ford drum brakes that are activated by a master cylinder and power booster hooked up to a Ford pedal assembly while at the front is a set of disc brakes hidden inside a set of those cool looking drum brake style covers with finned drums. They really suit the overall styling of the roadster. Bolted to the wheel flanges are billet

Roland's
Roadster

Words & Photos: Larry O'Toole

So-Cal Modified wheels that feature pin drives and hand made covers that replicate knock-off spinners from Vintage Engineering.

The GM engine was ditched in favour of a super looking Chrysler Hemi engine. This one is a real hot rodder's powerplant that has been bored by the Mopar Shop and fitted with balanced internals that include a Chrysler crank and NOS Chrysler con rods. Pistons are Ross Racing forged with a 10.5:1 compression ratio and fitted with Keith Black rings. The oil pump is from a small block 360 Mopar, the sump is a modified Milodon item fitted with a Hot Heads Research windage tray and the camshaft is an Isky activated by a Donovan gear drive with hydraulic lifters and steel Chrysler push rods. Sitting between those attractive Hemi heads is a NOS Moon intake manifold that mounts four Weber 48 IDA carburettors with injector-like air horns and the mixture they feed into the chambers is lit up by a Hunt magneto ignition. Adding to the attractiveness of the engine is a set of Donovan valve covers while all of the nuts, bolts, linkages and air horns are hand made to suit. An aluminium radiator takes care of cooling duties with assistance from an electric thermo fan and the exhaust features hand made three inch diameter glass pack mufflers.

Adapted to the back of the Hemi is a modified GM Turbo 350 automatic transmission with Lokar Classic shifter. Fuel supply is contained in a 45 litre original style '32 Ford tank and transferred to the engine by an electric pump.

The body for the hiboy came from Bott Rods and has been fitted with a flat steel firewall. The windshield is a modified Speedster style and the body is coated in straight black paint. Inside there is bright red pleated leather trim over a vintage bench seat with black carpet on the floor. The door panels are hand made with the same red leather as used on the seat. Stewart Warner gauges fill the dash panel and they are accompanied by a Moon tacho and hand made switches. Steering column is from Ididit with a modified steering wheel. Head and taillights are all original style '32 Ford items and the turn signals were pirated from a motorcycle, but the mirrors are more hand made items.

Roland stopped counting the overall cost a long time ago, but he was well rewarded by gaining a Top Ten award at the Euro Nats 2017, the first time the hiboy ventured out since completion.

CSRA

LEFT: Rear End Sunset - It's hard to focus on a beautiful rear end when the sun is in your eyes.

BELOW: Rocket - Two hot rods being pushed to the limit just to prove a point.

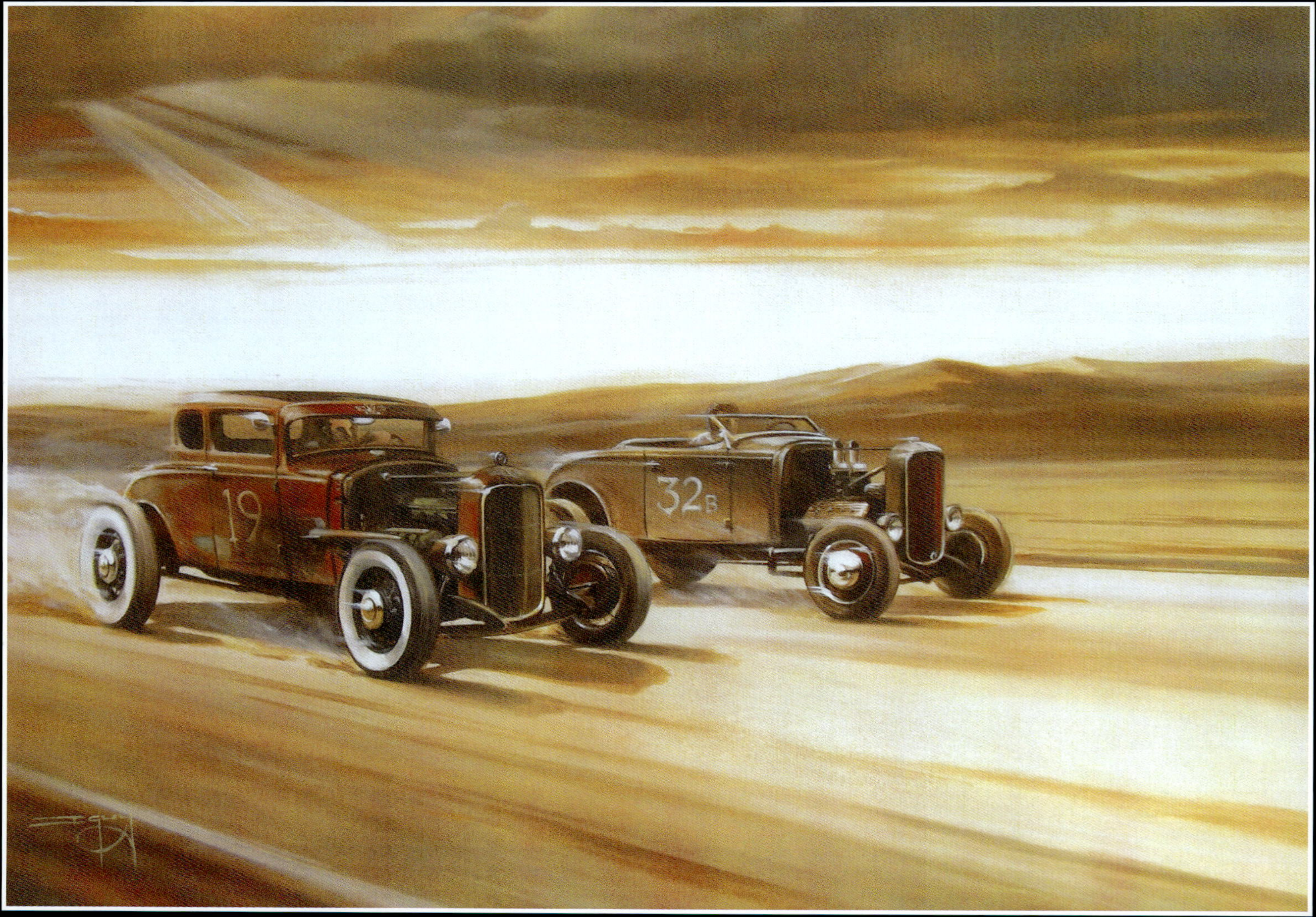

gallery

Ian Guy
Motoring Artist
Herefordshire, UNITED KINGDOM

"It's an artist's cliché but I have been drawing and painting since I was a kid, in my very early years I would disappear into whatever I was painting and become a part of a self made fantasy. You can imagine how this progressed through my childhood and teens, from Warner Bros and Disney through Marvel to the dark and dismal places you can only go as a troubled teen. Later my love of cars inspired a need to create long dusty roads for me to travel down, heading for a distant horizon, feeding my desire to escape.

Professionally I have always used oils on canvas. As I was growing up I shied away from colour. It wasn't somewhere I wanted to go. When I look back over quite a troubled childhood, I can see that I was creating a lot of very dark images in heavy black pencil on paper, colour wouldn't have lent itself kindly to my mood and what I was feeling and wanting to express. I think I drew myself out of a dark hole until I was ready to accept colour with a cautious embrace."

Now being established as a professional artist for over 30 years is something Ian Guy has difficulty coming to terms with.

"Time just goes by too quickly as you advance in years, and in the early days if you're struggling to make a living from your craft you don't even see it happening."

Having taken on commissions over the years both privately and corporately Ian now has a list of customers that will take him into 2020. A master of the finer details, that includes never missing a deadline, has led him to recently make the decision to stop taking on any more commissioned work for the foreseeable future.

"I just don't think it's fair to keep a customer waiting for so long and I see every commission as a gentleman's agreement which includes a one hundred percent commitment to deadlines for that special birthday, anniversary etc.

I will always be grateful for every commissioned piece, it's been a massive learning curve and the reason why I am where I am right now, it's a great feeling that someone has trusted me with something that is going to be so personal to them."

Ian moved south from where he was raised soon after his education, his idea being to sell art to tourists, something he had

ABOVE: Rear End Racers.

RIGHT: Salt and Dapper.

ABOVE: Sympathy for the Devil.
With an unmistakably huge influence from the cars of the Rolling Bones Hot Rod Shop no other name would suit this original artwork.

LEFT: Solitude.
At one with the salt, this Ford Model B roadster, the classic highboy hot rod, sits patiently on the salt flats, waiting.

RIGHT: Ian Guy with Jimmy Shine from So-Cal at Peterborough Hot Rod & Custom Show 2015.

been drawn to in his early teens whilst on holiday in Cornwall.

For many years Ian owned a public gallery in Saint Ives, Cornwall spending time painting local scenes, however his love of all things automotive often featured in his paintings and the success of an idea to incorporate a customer's car into the scene of their choice took off, leading him to try this same idea away from the gallery at various car shows and historic racing events. He soon realised being based so far south was becoming a hindrance and so decided to sell-up and move back "home" where he would be more centrally based. Looking back he says it was the best move he ever made.

Ian has admitted to having to incorporate the odd piece of original artwork into his busy schedule. He has images in his head that he just has to get out before normal progress can resume.

"With a commission every customer brings their own personal challenge, I strive not only to achieve the best result I can for them on canvas but also to create something that reflects who they are, I enjoy the building block, there is a certain discipline to it. When I do something for myself I am more likely to experiment with colour and light and I'm constantly learning, I find this exciting. My brush is constantly surprising me when I'm left to my own devices. I see it as two completely different things really, the second being more about learning and progression."

Ian says he's not quite sure what has happened over the last few years but a lot of his original work has sold whilst still in progress on the easel. "Maybe because I have little to offer in the way of choice, or it's just that people can see I'm getting more grey hair ha-ha!"

Ian has over 100 prints available to order direct from his website.

Unframed Prints at £25.00 with free shipping

Framed Prints at £59.00 including postage, UK only.

The website also provides a wealth of information about his techniques and demonstrates the development of a particularly detailed piece, from the earliest pencil drawings to the painting of the final brush strokes. It is refreshing and unusual to see a professional artist share his methods in this way.

www.motoringartist.com

RIGHT: Salt Flats.
Two classic hot rods, a '32 five window Ford Model B and a '34 Ford coupe.

BELOW: Deuce Coupe, Rear End, Salt Flats.
I'm not sure if this was a rat rod or a traditional rod being given a shake-down part way through its build.

BELOW: Throwing Salt.
With this painting I just wanted to capture two hot rods doing what they were built to do!

LEFT: Black Flamed Hot Rod. There's nothing much more iconic in the world of hot rods than a black 'n' flamed, chopped and fenderless, 1932 Ford Model B three window coupe.

BELOW: Little Red Coupe.

RIGHT: Storyteller.

LEFT: Gassed And Primed.
RIGHT: Road to Bonneville with the Duel Truck.
A classic '57 Chevy station wagon pulls a bellytank lakester on a home made trailer, heading for the holy grail of hot rodding, the Bonneville salt flats. While the menacing Peterbilt truck from the movie "Duel" makes its presence felt!
BELOW: Low Flyers - With this painting I really wanted to capture the feeling of speed and raw overwhelming power. Just as the boys, and girl, in their hot rods think they've reached the edge of a full adrenalin rush, suddenly from nowhere comes the almighty sound and overpowering presence of a B17 Flying Fortress bomber accompanied by a P51 Mustang and a P47 Thunderbolt. I hope this painting gives the viewer a little uneasy feeling and a slight urge to "duck"!

LEFT: Sonny Ray detail.

BELOW: Slingshot.

Pre-49 Street Rod

Photos & Words: Greg Stokes

ABOVE: Mark Holdaway's steel Deuce roadster runs genuine Ardun heads on the flathead and he drives it all over New Zealand.

MAIN: Mark Wilkin's Brookville bodied '32 Ford three window finished in two-tone blue runs an EFI Hemi and four-speed while Bruce Carter's candy green chopped '32 Ford three window is based on a Pete Osborne fibreglass body and runs a small block Chevy.

THE BIG TWO OH!

It was back in 1997 when the Mount Maunganui based Oceanside Street Rods hosted New Zealand's first Pre '49 Street Rod Nationals. The timing was perfect with a strong following of pre '49 American origin rodding in New Zealand that has only gone from strength to strength. Twenty years later Oceanside Street Rods once again hosted the event at the Wairakei Resort in Taupo, located in the central North Island of New Zealand, back in February 2017.

Like most things, the pre '49 movement in New Zealand has endured its share of politics and tall poppy syndrome. To be honest however, in the past twenty years a strong hot rod based industry has flourished in New Zealand because of the interest in pre '49 American origin vehicles. This was evident at the 20th anniversary event, attracting vehicles from all over the two islands including two cars visiting from the USA, not to mention the number of cool new cars debuting at the event.

This was the sixth time that Oceanside Street Rods had hosted the event that unfortunately was plagued with wet weather, ironically right in the middle of summer! The event kicked off with registration on Thursday night and Friday morning before a run departed to nearby Bruce McLaren Motorsports Park for some hot laps and car games. Fully catered meals and night time entertainment were all inclusive of the entrant fees and Saturday morning dawned another wet day for the show 'n' shine in Taupo, giving entrants the opportunity to please themselves for lunch and entertainment leading into the Saturday night awards function.

Time flies when you are having fun and Sunday morning included a cooked breakfast, Top Ten award winner's photos and final farewells. The 2018 event is in Nelson and is shaping up to be another neat weekend. If the past twenty years is anything to go by then the pre '49 movement in New Zealand has a strong future, with many cars being pro built, homebuilt or imported into New Zealand.

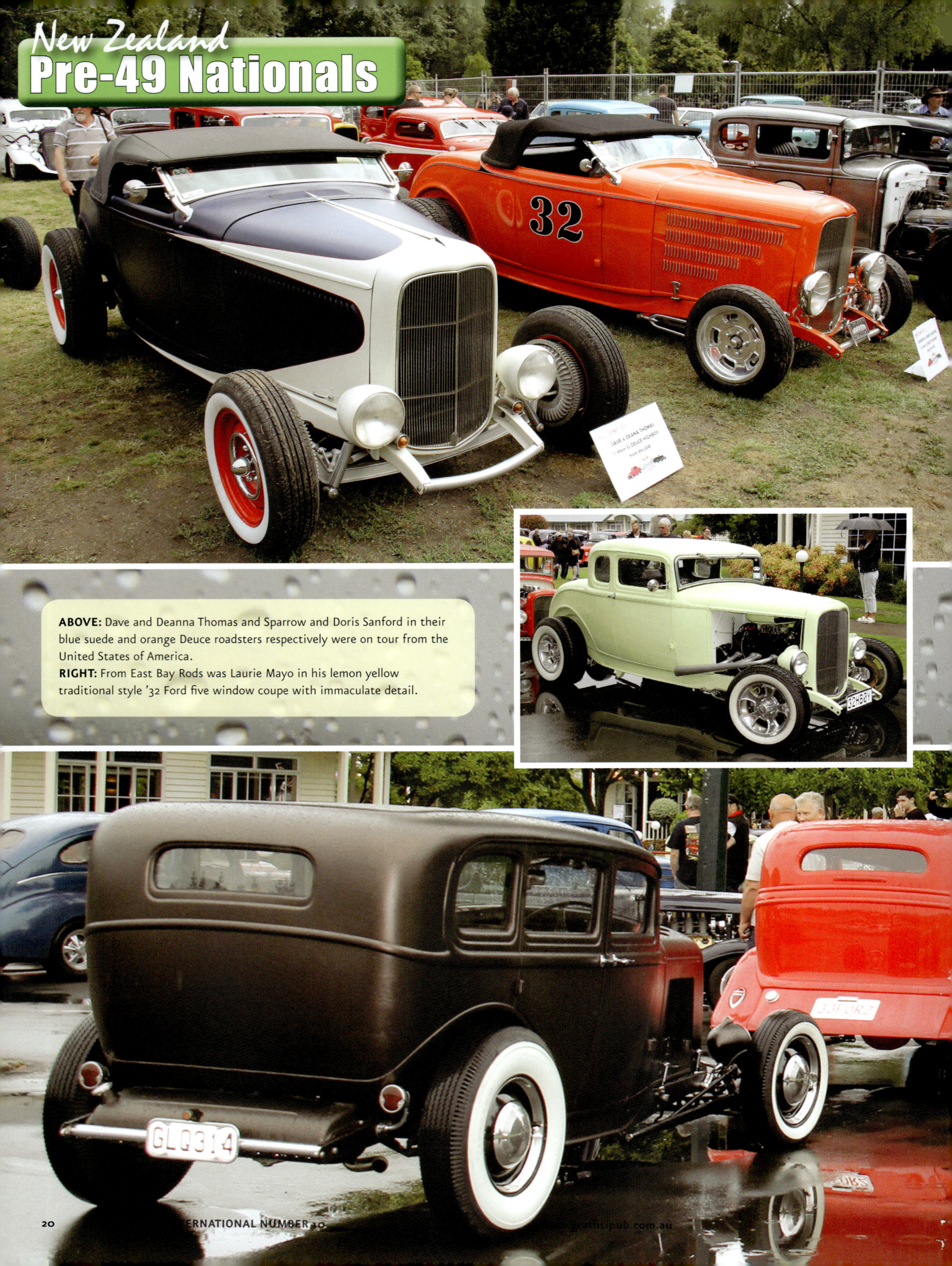

ABOVE: Dave and Deanna Thomas and Sparrow and Doris Sanford in their blue suede and orange Deuce roadsters respectively were on tour from the United States of America.
RIGHT: From East Bay Rods was Laurie Mayo in his lemon yellow traditional style '32 Ford five window coupe with immaculate detail.

RIGHT: New Zealand has a generous fender exemption law enabling cars like these Deuces to be driven anywhere, anytime.

BELOW RIGHT: Tania Foster's bare metal '36 Ford coupe and Alan Walker's '39 Chev dwarf the early Chev tourer between them.

ABOVE: Larry Barnett of Classic Cover Insurance drives this bare metal Model A coupe with a tri-carb small block Chev and five speed.
RIGHT: Peter Kidd's tasty '36 Ford three window coupe is the perfect addition to any rod run lineup.

ABOVE: It may have been raining throughout the weekend but New Zealand rodders weren't afraid to drive their cars on the rod run to the show and shine destination. Peter Farrant's brown suede '32 Ford sedan cuts a cool profile behind Bruce Carter's Rods by Reid built '33 Ford Tudor.

ABOVE: Sitting great going down the road is Chris Walton's tastefully restrained '34 Ford pickup from the Southside Streeters Club.

ABOVE: Master craftsman from the South Island, Rick Murray drove up in his totally handbuilt and unique Model A roadster pickup.

BELOW LEFT: Steve Flexman's glowing gold '36 Ford cabriolet features a well detailed flathead under the hood to round out the total '50s flavour.

BELOW: A hot rod with history is the chopped '34 Ford three window coupe of Marie Barberich that was rodded in the '70s by Dennis Stanley and called "Lollipop".

ABOVE: Woody Whitehouse's Model A roadster pickup, David Brown's Sam Foose built '40 Ford coupe, Ray Meharg's '37 Chevy coupe and Paul Servantie's '32 Ford sedan.

TOP LEFT: Nigel Oliver's Model A roadster was built at Rocket Speed Equipment with a small block Ford and four speed, plus a quick-change rear end.

TOP RIGHT: Noel Sutherland built up this '32 Ford roadster using the remains of the famous Lenny Jones roadster of the '60s and '70s.

ABOVE LEFT: Rick and Sue Dunn's '32 Ford Tudor ticks all the right boxes for hot rod style including Halibrand wheels and quick-change rear, Limefire headers and a Moon tank.

ABOVE: From Riverside Rodders, John Allen's owner-built '32 Ford coupe won Grand National Champion and Top Ten placings.

ABOVE: Having returned to New Zealand from Australia, Hank Robertson toured up from the South Island in this neat '34 Ford Tudor.

RIGHT: Bruce McKenzie's '41 Willys pickup is an outstanding vehicle with a blown big block Chev. It is currently being rebuilt after experiencing a road accident. Thankfully Bruce was unharmed.

ABOVE: Kevin Salter's Model A coupe, Dave Verry's '34 Ford coupe and Mark Homan's '41 Willys coupe.

BELOW LEFT: This was the "paddling pool" in the tray of Mark Stokes' Model A after one downpour of rain during the Friday!

BELOW LEFT: Ray Stephenson's Model A Tudor is striking in a light metallic copper hue.

BELOW RIGHT: First debuted in 1992 by John Reid, this Model A coupe dubbed "BILIT" still looks great under the ownership of Ian Taylor. The world class rod features milled billet aluminium throughout.

ABOVE: Weasel Davidson was one of a few who braved the elements with no top!

ABOVE RIGHT: Bare metal and rain don't go too well together. Regardless of that Mark Stokes still had fun in his Model A roadster pickup.

RIGHT: Ron Gubb is always building something different. This is his take on a '32 Ford roadster pickup.

MAIN: Line up of rods at the Pre '49 Street Rod Nationals.

BOTTOM: A Studebaker six cylinder is a cool and unusual powerplant choice as shown in Steve Montaperto's '32 Ford roadster.

Downscale Hot Rodding

ABOVE: I found this excellent Nomura tin-plate pickup in an Adelaide antique shop many years ago. There are several versions with different graphics including Pinkee the Farmer and John's Farm that have a load of chickens and eggs in the tray. The working V8 is a highlight.

ABOVE: This classic 1932 roadster is from around 1955 and produced in tin-plate by Nomura of Japan. Battery operated, the driver's head turns as it manoeuvres around randomly. Coloured lights on the engine flash and spark as it travels.

BELOW: Believe it or not, these toys are all related to the big blue Hubley roadster on the left. Size, materials, propulsion and even country of origin varies widely!

BELOW RIGHT: Judging by the finish on MS Toys' Hot Dog Rod, heavily patina'd rat rods are not such a new idea after all – it dates from the mid fifties. The original Hot Dog driver was a rather awkward looking tinplate canine. He yelped and rocked as you pushed the roadster along. My driver was missing but I found a replacement that came from a Hot Dog Shop playset – does that count?

Let's face it, if you are a hot rodder you like toys! And chances are, you liked toy cars when you were a kid. Growing up in Australia in the sixties, I would have said that there weren't many toy hot rods in the toy shops back then. The only one I can remember owning (I was about eight) was a little blue plastic fenderless tourer I bought at the local newsagent. Occasionally I would see a small Buddy L '36 Woody at Kmart but that was about it. Even though I built plastic models throughout my school years, I didn't get serious about collecting until my late 20s.

Like many I started collecting the 1/64th scale hot rods that Hot Wheels and others produced, but occasionally I would come across toy hot rods in different scales and materials. I remember naively thinking, "Hey, I might collect these – there's not that many of them!"

On my first visit to the USA, back in 1992, I started to get some idea of just how many toy hot rods were out there and after meeting a new friend, Dale, at the Louisville Nationals who collected toy Falcons, my collection took off. Over the next 20 years we swapped a box of hot rods for a box of Falcons. Good times! Then, in 1996 I met Bub Johnson, a rodder from Portland, Oregon who may just have had the best toy hot rod collection in the world. He graciously let me photograph his entire collection and that became my catalogue as I started collecting in earnest.

For me, toys are just that – toys that were made for kids to play with, on the floor, in the sandpit, or on the driveway. With that in mind, this article will just focus on toys, not the collectible 1/18th diecast rods you can buy these days at collector stores, department stores and car shows. I'm also going to steer away from the gazillions of Hot Wheels, Matchbox and similar 1/64th scale diecast – sure, they are toys, but we could fill this whole magazine just with those items.

At the risk of sounding like another episode of Sheldon Cooper's "Fun with Flags", I get a real kick out of tracking down the myriad toy hot

ABOVE: Over the years I have collected 47 different versions of Tonka Model As and their clones. They look right at home in this vintage Marx service station.

RIGHT: These large tinplate Model Ts were produced by the famous Japanese manufacturer Alps. They each appeared in three different versions with the wheels and colour schemes reflecting the changing trends over the years. Battery operated, the coolest feature is the smoke that steams out of the radiators as they drive along!

BELOW: Cragstan of Hong Kong battery powered remote control hot rod - two buttons for forward and reverse.

RIGHT: The proportions on this channelled roadster might be a bit elongated but the details on the flathead are exceptional for a tin plate toy.

BELOW: The Hot' See roadster was produced by Nosco Plastics of Erie Pennsylvania in 1952. The ingenious see-through four banger engine with a working piston assembly received a patent in 1955. Alongside is their Vizy Vee stock car that featured a V8 engine with similar working features.

rods that are out there. I love that there are so many, that they are made in so many sizes and materials, and in so many countries. I love seeing how hot rods are viewed through the eyes of non-hot rodders. Finally, I love comparing how they have evolved over the years, sometimes with one subject being reproduced by various manufacturers in different formats across several decades.

One thing I don't much care about is discussing their value. Something is only worth what you are prepared to pay for it and as I have no intention of selling them, the investment value is questionable. Internet auction sites do help you find some of these items, often with highly inflated prices, but there is no story. "I got it off eBay!" Hardly something to enthral the grandkids with, but when you discover something under a shelf in a dark antique store or buried with one wheel sticking up out of a sandpit, well then you've got a story!

What makes it a hot rod? For me, I stick with the generally accepted definition of pre-'49 and I expect to see at least big and little wheels or exposed engines, and typical roadster, coupe, and bucket body styles. If you have to explain to me that it is a hot rod, it probably isn't! On the other hand, I have been known to buy a "squintable" hot rod. What's squintable, I hear you ask? When you have to close one eye, and squint out of the other one, before you can just make out that it is a hot rod. Some toy hot rods exhibit beautiful proportions while other ones, well, they're squintable!

Hot rod toys can come from all over the world! There is a jacked up '38 Ford Standard coupe from Norway, a sandcast roadster from Fun-Ho in New Zealand, an overheating T sedan from Japan, a wind-up tin plate roadster from Korea, a clever mechanical '27 roadster from Schuco in Germany, a battery operated plastic '32 roadster from Hong Kong, a diecast full-fendered T bucket from England and even a tiny

cereal toy from Australia (that's the only commercially manufactured toy from Oz that I have been able to discover!). Naturally, with America being the home of the hot rod, it is also the home of the toy hot rod and a great number of them have been produced, especially in Illinois and Pennsylvania.

Even if we disregard the mass-produced diecast toys of the last few decades, there is still a neat range of diecast toy hot rods out there that date back considerably further. I guess the charm in these guys is that they are nowhere near as sophisticated as the ones we see on the racks today. Tootsietoy, Hubley and Midgetoy from the USA and Fun Ho from New Zealand produced quite a range of rods, but often they were a simple one piece casting with all detail moulded in. Little or no plastic was added other than the wheels.

Buddy L, Tonka and Nylint are American companies that specialised in stamped steel toys, rugged enough for outdoor play. Although they are best known for their yellow trucks and earthmoving toys, in the sixties they produced some terrific hot rods as well. They are easy to find at on-line auction sites and they are excellent candidates for stripping down, repainting and customising, using full size bodywork techniques and materials. I've redone four of mine and love them as much as the originals. In the seventies Tonka and Buddy L also made ranges of smaller sized toys with considerably more plastic in them.

I find it fascinating when toy companies from around the world make copies of someone else's toy or model. The Hubley '32 roadster (yeah, I know, it's more like a '27 T roadster if you squint enough) is a prime example of this. Hubley made their model in around 1/20th scale as a diecast kit in 1960. The famous German mechanical toy company, Schuco, then made a very cool tin-plate and diecast toy with a wind-up mechanism and posable steering. Cragstan of Hong Kong then did a medium size copy of the car as a battery operated plastic toy with wire wheels and a driver.

Another legendary American toy company, Tootsietoy, managed

RIGHT: This preloved Nomura roadster known as the Lightning Hot Rod has a nicely proportioned body. Toys in this condition do not command as high a price as mint originals, making them more accessible. I'm using a substitute engine and driver's head until a better example comes along.

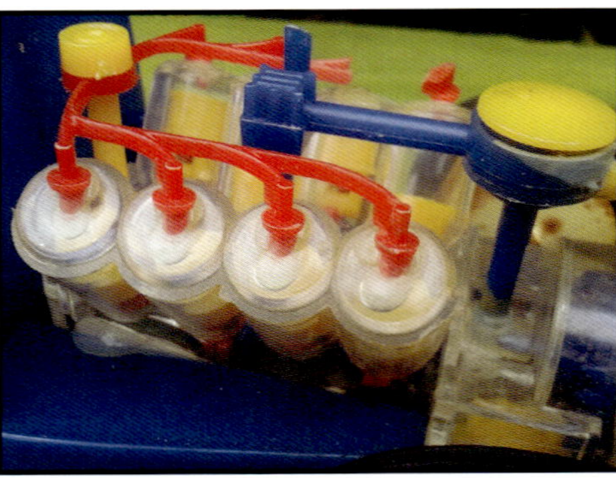

LEFT & ABOVE: Two multi-coloured cruisers enjoy their multi-coloured roadster with a snappy Buick styled grille. Nosco mixed and matched the red, blue and yellow parts to produce three different colour schemes for each toy. The front axle drives a gear that in turn drives the crankshaft and pistons. A friction type motor provided the motive power for this toy car.

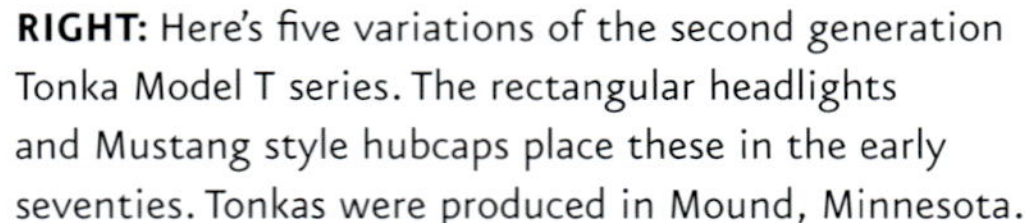

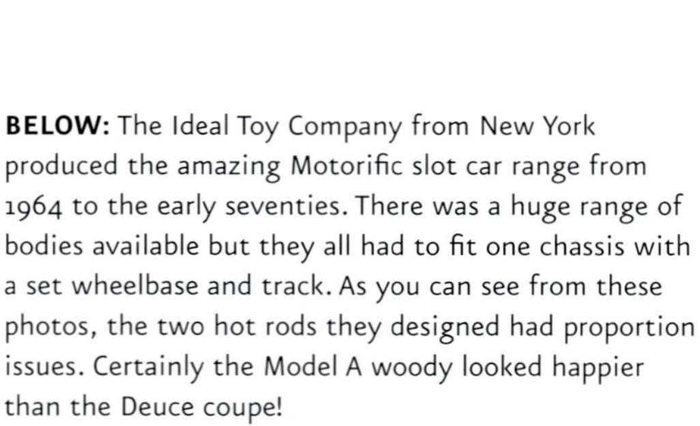

RIGHT: Here's five variations of the second generation Tonka Model T series. The rectangular headlights and Mustang style hubcaps place these in the early seventies. Tonkas were produced in Mound, Minnesota.

BELOW: The Ideal Toy Company from New York produced the amazing Motorific slot car range from 1964 to the early seventies. There was a huge range of bodies available but they all had to fit one chassis with a set wheelbase and track. As you can see from these photos, the two hot rods they designed had proportion issues. Certainly the Model A woody looked happier than the Deuce coupe!

BELOW RIGHT: These two Deuces (if you squint) come from the American Flyer slot car set made by AC Gilbert of Connecticut. They are perhaps better known for their Erector sets and model trains. They also did a '40 Ford coupe as a stock car and all were in approximately 1/48th scale.

ABOVE: When we talk of hybrid cars today, we are probably thinking petrol/electric rather than T-bucket/Austin Healey! That appears to be the design philosophy behind Irwin's hot rod for Barbie, Ken and Midge dolls. To let the passengers sit comfortably in the car, the engine is hollowed out so that Barbie's long legs fit inside. This 1963 toy is by far the largest one in my collection.

ABOVE: Tonka's first range of Model T based rods appeared in two different sizes but with very similar proportions. Note that the colour schemes and engines are the same on these two, but the larger one has whitewall tyres.

to come up with a cheap and cheerful diecast version around 1/43rd scale. It's lost a bit in the translation, but the Offy style engine and the slightly odd Deuce grille gives away its origins. Meanwhile a very cool tin-plate version, identified only by "Made in Japan", features the Hot Rod magazine logo. Although the proportions have changed somewhat, you can still see the Hubley bones of this toy. Not long ago, Schuco made a tiny diecast replica of its earlier mechanical toy, in its Piccolo range. Recently I thought I saw yet another clone of the Hubley roadster – who knows how many other ones there are? Clones are simply one of those quirks that I love hunting down for my collection.

The next category we will look at is the soft plastic toys that I refer to as sandpit toys. Often with a one piece body with minimal extra parts, maybe a steering wheel, driver or windscreen frame but that's about it. The wheels and axles usually snap onto mounts protruding from the body shell. That blue tourer I mentioned in my opening paragraph – that was a sandpit toy.

Like all good toys, it has a story. It disappeared as I grew into a teenager, as toys often do. I had managed however, to save the removable rear seat, thinking I might use it on a model one day. On my first trip to the USA, we stopped in a 7-Eleven store to get some food and I spotted two red toy roadster pickups on the shelf. They were 40 cents each! I don't remember why but I decided to kneel down and see if there were any more on the floor under the shelf. Lo and behold, there was a red tourer, the same toy as my childhood blue one from 30 years previous, but MISSING ITS SEAT! I couldn't wait to get home to snap in the blue seat and make it complete – it wouldn't be the same story if the seat had been red! Later, in a box of toys passed on by my brother, I found the stripped body of a roadster version of the same toy. I swapped out the missing parts from the second roadster pickup to give me all three

versions. Oddly enough, some versions known as Dune Runners get a set of sand paddle tyres and they all feature a chromed clip-on engine casting.

Most of the soft sandpit toys are roadsters and many of them are red. That suits me just fine! (I built a Hennarot Red '29 Model A roadster from various accumulated parts, first licensed in 1984, and it has been my beloved daily driver ever since.) The two Model A roadsters I have, however, are yellow and blue – not red! There is also a very cool '34 five window coupe and a much smaller '36 three window coupe, both in a bunch of colours. In the nineties there was also a very large '34 roadster that hit Australian shops and it looks like it might be a clone of the Solido 1/18th diecast model.

Hard plastic toys were a feature of the Hong Kong toy industry in the sixties and seventies. Zee Toys and Lucky Toys are typical brand names but many have no manufacturers' names on them at all. Some of them can be quite nicely detailed and proportioned, but the nature of the plastic means that they are often found in a broken state. They will respond to conventional plastic model making techniques when it comes to repair and in the past I have even converted some of them into detailed scale models – 1/25th was a popular scale for these toys.

For a major increase in rarity, consider the tether car. These were toys for older kids, and typically were based on a cast aluminium shell powered by a single cylinder glow-plug model plane engine. The scene back in the forties and fifties was comparable with the radio/control racing hobby today. The cars ran around circular tracks and were timed for top speed – they were tethered with wire to a pole in the centre of the track, thus explaining their name. The hobby flourished in Australia and there are some well-known Aussie rodders with respectable collections out there. The value of these has escalated

RIGHT: These are the three Model A rods originally released by Tonka, I'm guessing in the early to mid-sixties. At this stage they were mostly stamped steel bodies and fenders with plastic seats and details.

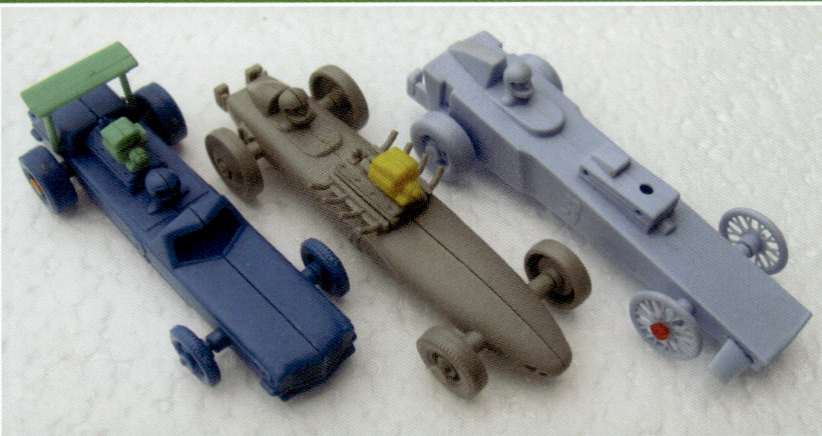

ABOVE: These three dragsters were made in Melbourne and were found in cereal boxes in the sixties. They often came in a large variety of colours as can be seen in my mixed and matched collection.

ABOVE RIGHT: These two sand cast aluminium roadsters were made in Inglewood, New Zealand by Fun-Ho. The re-issued blue version has Buddy L wheels and tyres simply because Fun-Ho bought a quantity and used them at the time.

ABOVE, LEFT & BELOW: Not quite toys but I really wanted you guys to see these Christmas decorations. Some are blown glass, the more recent ones are highly finished plastic but they are all very cool. Where else are you going to find a fenderless '34 four door sedan?

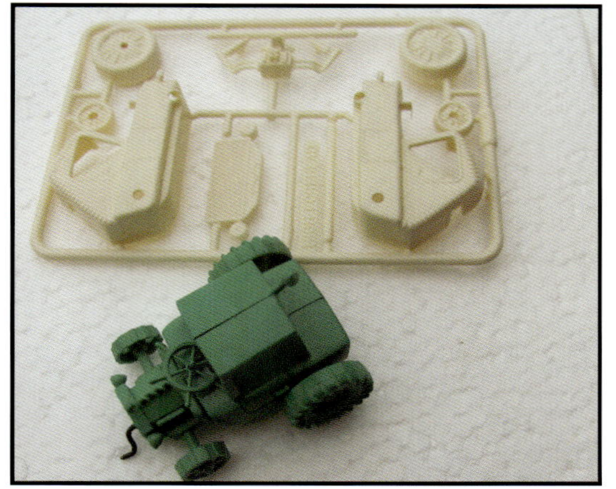

LEFT & RIGHT: Cereal toys were very popular in the sixties and seventies, miniature model kits that came on a small plastic frame that slid down the side of the cornflakes, Weeties or whatever you had for breakfast. They are as fragile as a potato chip so finding one in any condition at all is challenging!

LEFT & RIGHT: These two plastic roadsters were made by Marx (r) and Saunders Tool & Die Company of Aurora, Illinois (l). They both date back to around 1950. The Marx roadster has a friction motor that when pushed along generates sparks under the transparent red rocker cover of its straight eight engine – a pretty neat feature for a toy of this age.

considerably over the years and even an entry level car will punch a hole in your wallet!

The king of toy hot rods must surely be the tin plate toy. Some of them have survived fifty years or more but, as with all toys, condition is everything. These things can be expensive and you are not just competing with hot rod collectors, you are competing with toy collectors in general. Fortunately there were a lot of them made so pre-loved examples can be found in very displayable condition. These were originally produced in the fifties and sixties, often in Japan but other Asian countries as well as America, England and Germany also produced them. While modern repro tin plate toys in general can be found in toys shops and markets around the country, I haven't found any repro tin plate hot rods - yet.

The nature of their production with lithographed ink decoration on a stamped tin plate body, means that they sometimes exhibit slightly odd proportions, not helped by the fact that few people in their country of origin had ever seen a real one! Nevertheless they have a certain charm and hold an important place in my collection. It is also common for them to be battery operated with mystery action, moving engine parts or some other unique play feature. I am just as happy to get a cheap one that is play worn and missing a few parts as I am to step up for a truly mint boxed version.

I mentioned earlier that Tonka had a range of smaller sized Model A Ford based toys. Tonka themselves updated and modified these

many times over the years. Obviously many other toy companies were impressed with the Tonkas because they did their own cloned versions, sometimes even copying the colours and sticker designs. My Tonka (and related) Model A collection now runs to 47 different cars and I know I don't have them all yet!

Cereal toys were very popular in the sixties and seventies, miniature model kits that came on a small plastic frame that slid down the side of the cornflakes, Weeties or whatever you had for breakfast. Excavation of these treasures could be messy but still worth a backhander from Mum if you beat your (in my case, three also car nuts) brothers to it. A lot of these were made in Australia so if my sources are correct, these little hot rods may be the only Australian made hot rod toys in my collection. They're special for that fact alone! Problem is, they are as fragile as a potato chip so finding one in any condition at all is challenging! And venturing outside our hot rod definition for a moment, they even did a very credible version of an AP6 Valiant station wagon and an XP Falcon sedan. Good luck finding them today!

And now for something completely different – Christmas decorations. Not quite toys but I really wanted you guys to see these things. Some are blown glass, the more recent ones are highly finished plastic but they are all very cool. Where else are you going to find a fenderless '34 four door sedan?

Even though sports cars and Grand Prix cars make up the majority

RIGHT: After many years and many variations those original Model As morphed into these outrageous Roth T shirt style caricatures. I found one of these in Perth and two in the States.

ABOVE: These three hot rods belong to a series made by Clover Toys in Korea. The crank handle fires up the friction motor inside. My lovely wife insists the orange one is based on a 2CV Citroen, which I have a bit of trouble coming to terms with. Who does such a thing?!

LEFT: I know almost nothing about this toy except that it is in mint condition and is the only one I have ever seen anywhere! A big win off eBay, it features some sort of spring loaded arrangement that causes it to explode into pieces on impact. Great fun but I am too scared to try it out. It was called an action puzzle toy that retailed for 98c.

ABOVE: Cragstan produced a large range of these Model A based hot rods. I originally thought I had found rare hiboy versions only to discover that they had simply been hot rodded by a previous owner. Buyer beware!

ABOVE: This plastic T tourer by Playart from Hong Kong appears to be inspired by the Tonka Model Ts and yet Tonka didn't have a tourer in its range. Playart also did a roadster to accompany the tourer.

ABOVE: The spirit of post war track roadsters is beautifully captured in this diecast toy by Midgetoys from Rockford Illinois. I replaced the damaged wheels on the silver version with those from a Maisto Tonka truck diecast.

RIGHT: From West Hempstead, Long Island, Aurora is a well known maker of plastic kits. While this red plastic roadster is indeed a kit, its large size, clunky scale detailing, working lights and electric motor blurs the line between model and toy. The box art clearly shows a '29 Model A roadster body but this 1960 release is called a 1932 Ford Custom Hot Rod.

BELOW: From left to right, a Tootsietoy '32 style roadster, a Toosietoy '40 Ford Convertible, Marx '36ish three window coupe, a Hubley '34 three window parked in front of a Mettoy tinplate dolls house from Great Britain dating back to 1954.

of subject matter for slot car manufacturers, there has been a fair sampling of hot rods over the years. Eldon made a great trio in 1/48th scale of a '36 roadster, '27 T pickup and an early version of the legendary Lil' Coffin but sadly I have never found any affordable examples! The Gibert's American Flyer racing set included two rather oddly proportioned Deuces, a coupe and a roadster. Aurora has some great Model As in its lineup from the seventies, but like all slot cars, they are going to cost you dearly unless you get lucky.

Most of the cars described here were manufactured in the fifties, sixties and seventies, but don't for a minute think that they don't make toys like that any more! Toy companies still routinely produce hot rods – only this week I spotted a three inch long roadster in BigW with Mickey Mouse at the wheel. Remember, everything old today was new yesterday, so there is no time like today to start a toy hot rod collection.

I've been collecting seriously for nearly thirty years and while my collection has grown significantly in that time there are two things I know for sure. First, I don't have every toy hot rod there is and second, I probably never will! That's a good thing, because it keeps me looking, never knowing what's lurking in the next antique shop, garage sale or (if I'm desperate) online auction. I love having the only example I've ever seen of a toy and yet I still love seeing toys in other people's collections that I don't have. I have plucked toys out of a mate's shed (sorry Michael!), kid's toy boxes (sorry Ben – not the only one – tragic, I know), and even found one at the store of a fast food chain that I'd never eaten at before.

Considering how little vintage tin any of us manage to spot in the wild these days, vintage toys have filled the void for me. I'd much rather bring these puppies home from a trip than souvenir teaspoons or snow domes! To me, these are just as cool an addition to any rodder's shed as enamel signs, oil cans or drive-in speakers. You just have to keep searching – good luck and happy hunting!

ABOVE & BELOW: The right hand drive Fun Ho aluminium roadsters have obviously been modified from the Auburn rubber version with left hand drive. Auburn Rubber toys were made in Auburn Indiana between 1935 and 1969. This hot rod roadster comes in a variety of colours and with different numbers moulded on the doors. The engine appears to be an inline six.

OLD CAR CITY
The Photographer's Paradise!

Words and Photos: Al O'Toole

In White, Georgia just off US Highway 411, lies an epic automotive graveyard known as Old Car City USA. The property has been in the same family since 1931, when current owner, Dean Lewis' parents opened the original building as a general store. During the forties the woodlands around the store were used as a junkyard for scrapping cars and by the end of the decade, the Lewis' had accumulated quite a collection. Eventually the family's focus shifted more towards running the store and the scrapyard was left to decay. Dean took over the business in 1970 and dreamed that one day, the family's junkyard would be opened as a museum for the general public to tour.

Thick vegetation covering more than 34 acres is slowly swallowing over 4400 vehicles of all makes and models and to walk the entire six miles of trails that intertwine these relics takes a full day. The main building and its immediate surrounds are littered with folk art and vintage collectables and while there are many desirable and salvageable cars throughout the property, none of them, or their parts are for sale. It's kind of heartbreaking really, but it truly is a photographer's paradise!

ABOVE: Late '30s Ford Tudor has the remains of another one for company.
ABOVE LEFT: Split window VW Kombi is a valuable vehicle these days, but this one is well on its way to oblivion.
BELOW: Front on view of a '41 Ford shows broken diecast grille and evidence of rust in the lip of the hood.

MAIN PIC: Top of the old van is a '55 Chevy two door post while the rare '65 Plymouth Barracuda in the foreground still has its massive rear glass intact.

BELOW LEFT: Ford pickup trucks are '56 F100 stepside at the left and a '48 F1 stepside on the right.

BELOW RIGHT: Another Ford pickup on the left, this time a '55 model in company with a '48 GMC.

ABOVE: Two of Ford's compact models from the sixties. On top is '63 Fairlane, underneath is '62 Mercury Comet.

ABOVE: Now this is rare and desirable. Unfortunately rust has got the better of a '49 Oldsmobile convertible.

BELOW: Cadillacs to the left, Fords to the right. The Caddy at left appears to be a '48 model while the one at right is a '52, both four door sedans. The Fords are '52 on the left and '55 on the right. Despite the rust damage, most vehicles in the yard have lots of intact stainless steel trim pieces still in place.

ABOVE: More Cadillacs, starting at left with a '63, next is '56, and at the right is a '58. The shrubbery is winning!

ABOVE: Time for a Studebaker, this one a '53 Commander coupe as is popular for dry lakes racing due to the swoopy body style.

RIGHT: There's even some early tin like these Model A coupe pieces stacked against a fence. They belong to a '30-'31 model.

ABOVE: Studebaker fans can collectively sigh now. On the right is a '52 model. next is '50 bullet nose sedan and the third example is a '53 sedan.

BELOW: What a customiser couldn't do with those taillights and stainless steel trim! Underneath all the foliage is a swoopy '57 Lincoln Premiere coupe.

RIGHT: It's not all cars at Old Car City, check out the yard art aeroplane keeping company with a Jeep and a Cadillac.

BELOW: Imagine this '64 Galaxie Country Squire wagon in pristine condition and equipped with air-bag suspension.

ABOVE: Amongst the later model cars in Old Car City is this '66 Pontiac GTO that would have come standard with a 389 V8 engine.
BELOW: Mostly complete '50 Ford two door sedan seems destined to miss out on a new lease of life as a custom.

ABOVE: There isn't lots of early tin amongst the wrecks but these pieces are mostly to suit '30 Model A closed cab pickups.
BELOW: Not many of these appear to have survived, it's a '65 Imperial Crown Coupe with tree embedded between bumper and grille.

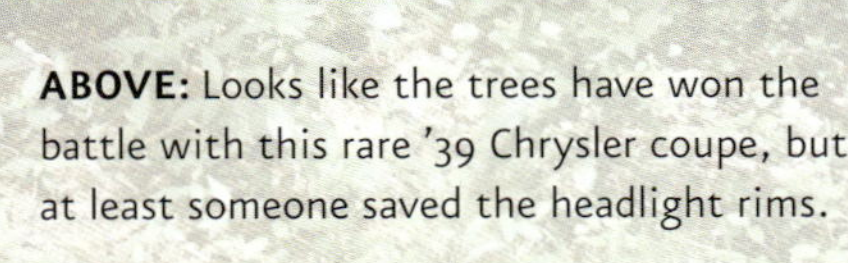

ABOVE: Looks like the trees have won the battle with this rare '39 Chrysler coupe, but at least someone saved the headlight rims.

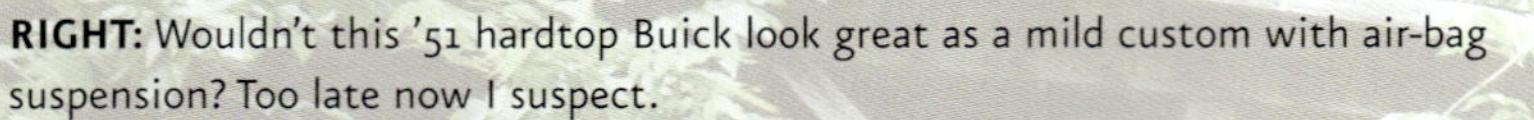

ABOVE: The near car is a '53 Packard Club sedan, described by the factory as the prestige car of the medium priced field. On the far side is a '54 Kaiser, the next to last model for the Kaiser company.

ABOVE: The body looks to be in good shape but this '48 Chevy coupe has been signed all over the front half. This one is obviously in better condition because it has been kept under cover.

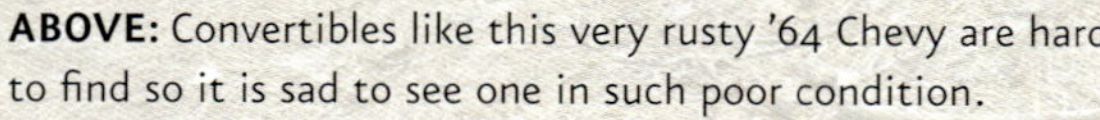

ABOVE: Convertibles like this very rusty '64 Chevy are hard to find so it is sad to see one in such poor condition.

ABOVE: Fighting for space with the ever pervasive trees is a '54 Ford on the left and a '39 DeSoto four door sedan on the right.

ABOVE: The headlight rim identifies this Lincoln Zephyr as a '40 model, the first to use sealed beams.

BOTTOM: The four door hardtop styling and what was called the T-Bird roofline indicates this '59-1/2 Ford is a Galaxie version.

BELOW: Last year of the big fins, combined with heavy stainless trim, were these decorative monsters on the '60 Plymouth Belvedere sedan.

Cord Limey!

Andy Saunders takes custom car building to another level

1936
CUSTOM
CORD

CUSTOM

RED BUS

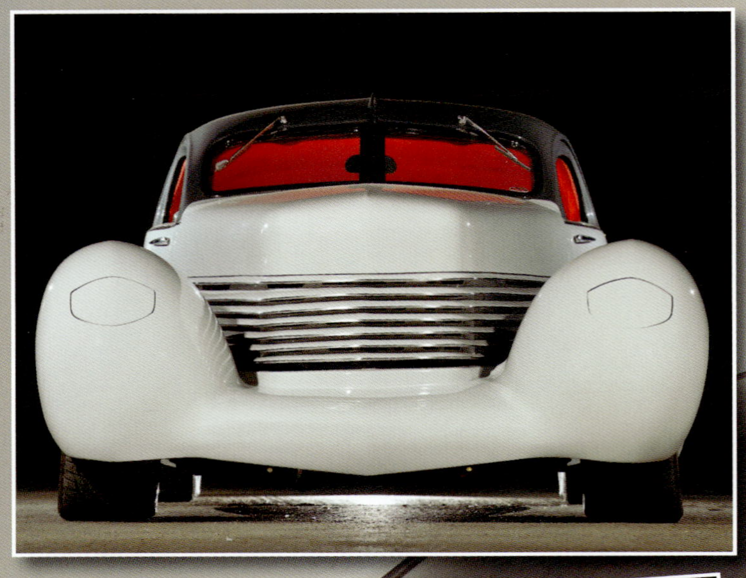

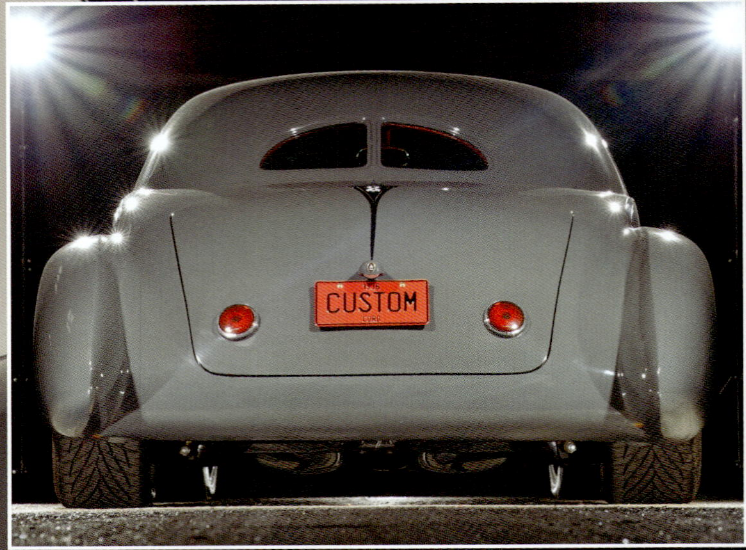

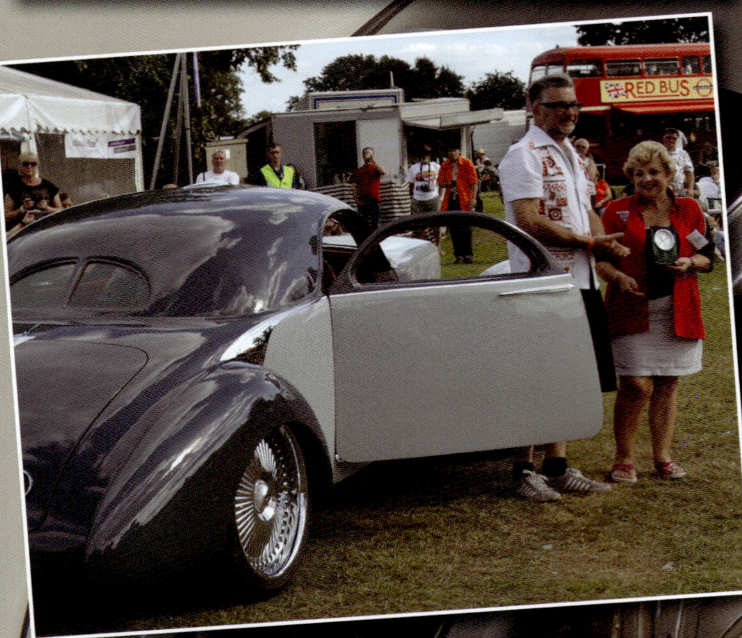

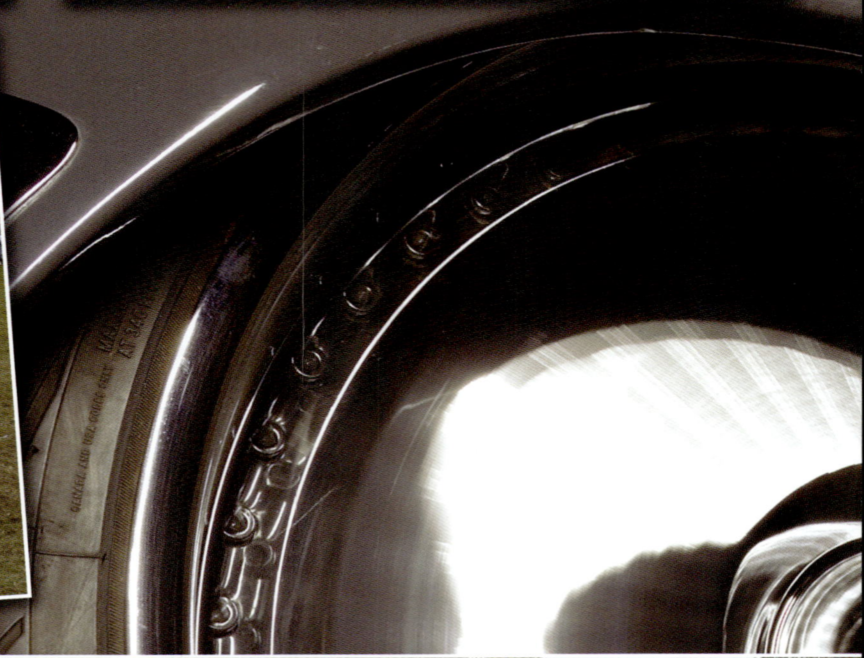

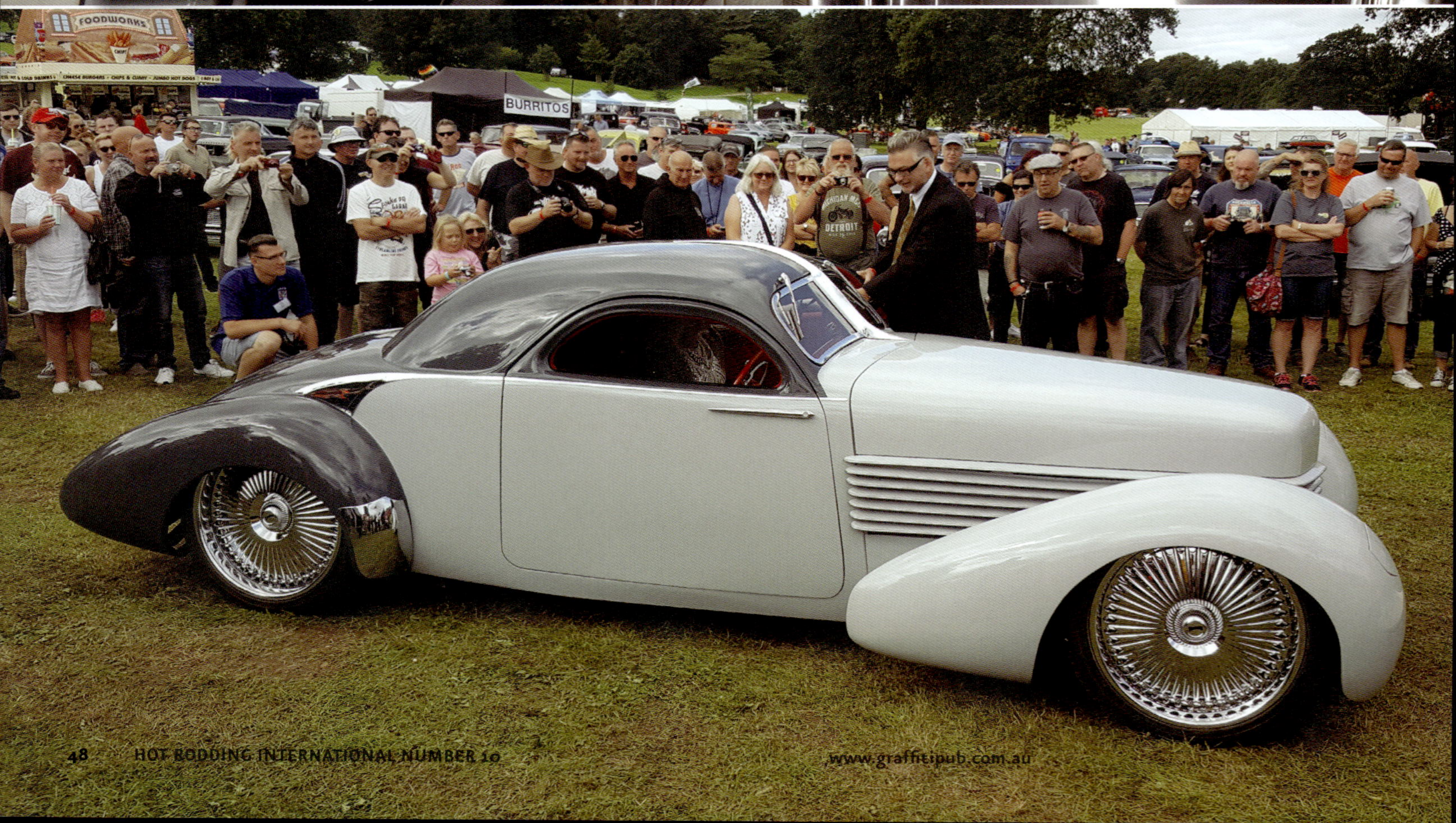
FOODWORKS
BURRITOS
DETROIT

In the latter half of the 20th century, there were plenty of famous British hot rod builders. All of them brought new levels of skill, vision and superlative engineering to the game, pushing the boundaries of how hot rods should look, and one-upping each other on how close to perfection they could achieve. However, I'd argue that there was only one British custom builder in the same league. You ask ten people on the scene who the most prolific, most famous and most accomplished custom builder on the scene is, and I reckon nine of them will give you the same answer: Andy Saunders, a guy who didn't so much push the boundaries as decide that there are no boundaries, and that the rules can go and get buggered.

Over the years, Andy has created some truly game-changing machinery. However, a couple of years ago, the Saunders' lock-up, that would normally be thrumming like Santa's workshop, went quiet. A combination of body blows in Andy's personal life led him to close the garage door and turn his back on everything, and while he never actually relinquished his crown, it did go into storage for a while.

Fortunately for all of us, his long-missing Mojo returned recently, and, with crown firmly re-ensconced upon his royal bonce, what better way to dive back into the thick of things than with the part-started project he'd bought in 2003?

If you're going to stage a comeback, you want to stage a BIG comeback, and Andy's choice of base vehicle was always going to stop folks in their tracks – a 1937 Cord 812, one of a mere handful that left the Auburn factory as right-hand drive. These Buehrig-penned beauties were the last word in late Art Deco styling, and boasted such cutting-edge tech as a Lycoming V8 driving the front wheels through a semi-automatic transmission. These coffin-nose Cords command silly money in restored condition, and even a scabby survivor will fetch $50,000 telling you everything you need to know about Andy's example, that set him back £500.

This particular car was sold new through RSM Automobiles on Berkeley Square, the UK's sole Auburn and Cord concessionaire, and the first owner was the Earl of Derby. Starting off so high up the social ladder, however, just meant that this Cord had farthest to fall, and by the time the new century rolled around, it had fallen just as far as it could. It was still in the possession of the wealthy and landed, but lay forgotten in a shed. The owner had bought it some 20 years previously with the intention of restoring it, rapidly realised he'd bitten off more than he could chew and put it up for sale. It stayed for sale for 20 years... which, again, tells you all you need to know. Then, in stepped Mr Saunders.

"My mate Graham told me about the car at the Rally Of The Giants, at Knebworth in 2003," says Andy. "I went to have a look, and the owner's mother opened the garage door... it wasn't worth saving. It was covered in rubbish, and parked tight up against a wall. I offered her £500. She replied that it was a Cord, and worth far more than that, and in fact she had the valuations chappie from Bonhams coming to view it that week for their upcoming "unrestored" auction. So I left. That week, she called me back and asked if the offer still stood. Apparently, the chap from Bonhams had been and told her it was "unfair to try to remove it from its resting place!"

"I collected the car on the weekend of the NSRA Supernats. On arrival, I opened the door of the garage to shove it out and Colin Ware exclaimed 'I'm not touching that before I've had a f**king tetanus!' And thus the car was named. We put it on the trailer, aerosoled Andy Saunders' New Project,' on it, and went straight to the Supernationals. When we got there, I prised the bonnet open, and that's when I realised... there's no gearbox at the front. Instead, there was a Ford flathead, a transmission that had been gas-axed through the bulkhead, a prop inside the cabin and an Austin back axle! I couldn't understand."

"The lady had told me that the second owner was a stock car racer, Jerzy Wójtowicz, a decorated WWII pilot who had escaped Poland to fly for the RAF. After the war, he got into stock car racing, and was world champion; Steve Corbett sent me some flyers from Ipswich track in the fifties, and this guy was top of the bill, a huge star. Apparently he'd picked the car up after the war with a failed gearbox. Cord had gone bankrupt in 1937, and spares were unavailable, meaning that this 10-year-old car was just about worthless, so he built it for racing. Then, one of two things happened – I heard he'd moved to Australia and died soon after, then I've also heard that

he didn't die until 2002, but either way, the car was never raced. It was just left in a field in Yorkshire to disintegrate, and for the local kids to jump all over, until this lady's son bought it in the eighties.

"As soon as I got home from the Supernationals, I began stripping it. It was definitely too far gone to restore – the passenger side door locks were rusted solid shut, and the interior could give you diseases. I hit the front passenger door with a lump hammer until it opened, but on hitting the passenger rear door, the B-pillar with both doors attached fell out, taking the roof gutters and door shuts with them. I hadn't noticed until then that the B-pillar was so rusty that the bottom four inches were missing, and it was attached to the sill by a lump of 4"x2" wood that had crumbled away. That's when I decided that it had to be a coupe as there was no chance of keeping it a four-door. It's an all steel body, but it was all rotten, and whatever you touched just turned into a shower of flakes. I just swept it up and carried on. Even my Dad said 'What have you bought that for?' I replied that it was only £500, and he told me that was £490 too much."

"The lower five inches of the bonnet had rusted away; I've never seen a single-skin panel rust like that. There were no return lips left on the arches, no grille, and the two vents on top of the scuttle had rusted into one huge hole and fallen in, meaning that the rain had poured in on the back of the dash! Had this car been anything other than a Cord, I wouldn't have even bothered with it, I wouldn't have contemplated dragging it home.

"These were one of the first monocoque cars, but had huge 6"x9" chassis members from the axle forward, and a huge front subframe that bolts on. We lifted what was left of the body into the back of a pick-up and sent it for shotblasting, which dissolved all the bits that looked good! Not much came back – just the roof, the pillars on one side, the rear inner arches, and part of the scuttle. I'd already cut the floors out, and the firewall was cut away years ago for the flathead, so the first job was to make and weld in some inner and outer sills just to put some strength back into the shell and join front and back.

"I went to the scrap-yard and bought a written-off XJ40, thinking I could just use the whole floorpan, but the configuration was wrong so it wouldn't have worked, and wouldn't have looked nice if it did. Instead, I cut the floorpan out from the rear seat backwards and welded that in, complete with rear axle and boot floor. The front clip is from a MkII Jaguar, that Dave Harries installed and triangulated."

"When I first started, I kept a tally of the expenses, and the first three items were the purchase of the car, bunging my mate £100 to drag it home, then buying those wheels. Yes, I bought those wheels back in 2003, as even back then I knew which way the build would go – they've got rust specks on them now! I saw these Dub Spin Bellagio wheels in Lowrider magazine and thought they looked very thirties and quite elegant. It was the most nervous purchase I've ever made – they were quite expensive, and the guy I ordered them from in California sounded like he was off his face... I bolted them on, then built the car around the wheels."

"I repaired the bonnet, the scuttle and the front wings. Originally, this car would have had the 812 grille with the holes for the exhausts, but that was long gone so I bought a 1936 810 grille without the holes. It's all one piece, so the people I bought it from in the US cut it in half to ship it and I welded it back together at this end. I swapped the front brakes for the vented discs and calipers from an XJ12, which widened the track by four inches, so I had to pie-cut the inside edge of the wings to stretch it over the wheels. The Cord had a strange, ugly chin piece to cover the gearbox, which I didn't have and didn't want, so I redesigned the front valance area to be much sleeker.

"The doors were made using the original front door skins and part of the rear skin, with the lower six inches replaced using Mini repair panels, and the inner frames made almost from scratch. Cord made a two-door roadster called the Sportsman with doors 7.75" longer than the sedan's, and I wanted to make it as much like a roadster as possible so I copied that. The B-pillars were made from 2x2 box, and the hinges were forged steel household items, but hanging the doors to sit correctly and open without touching the rear quarters or sills took weeks."

CUSTOM

"The rear quarters were handmade by an amazing panel beater called Roy Dean, who passed away three years ago at the age of 87, and was panel beating until the week before he died. Ron was the guy who made the rear arches for my step-side Escort (My first SM feature car back in 1981) and also the roof for 'Indecision'. The rear panel between the window and the boot is part of a VW Beetle roof skin whilst the boot lid and surround are 1961 MkII Jaguar with the ugly number plate hump removed. The taillights are Cord repro whilst the number plate light is the original.

The rear wings were made 10" over length to follow the shape of the fronts. There was nothing left of the nearside wing, and only the front section of the offside; Ron just made the rest. The original A-pillars were the only good, solid part of the car, so we chopped them three inches – I've still got the sections we cut out – and built everything from there back by eye. The screen frames are aluminium reproductions from Auburn Cord Duesenberg Parts in Kansas, who were really helpful. I chopped the frames and Ron oxy-welded them back together, with no soap! There was only one tiny imperfection, so I chromed the frames, leaving the imperfection there to remind me what a clever guy Ron was. The screens still open; they go almost horizontal. The rear screen on the sedan is only about 15° from vertical, so I cut it out and raked it until it flowed right.

"Once the rear window and boot were in place, I made the rear valance and seam-welded it all. There must be 600 feet of welding in that shell. Once I realised what I was doing, I thought it would be the best car I'd ever created, so it'd have to be straight. We leaded the roof all over, then used U-Pol metal filler, which is the hardest thing ever to rub down, it's like concrete. Then a coat of stopper, then U-Pol Reface… perfect. I'd decided early on that it would be two-tone. I'd taken my Mum to a garden centre, and walked past a carousel of birthday cards. One card had three or four cartoon cars, one of which was an Art Deco-style car in two-tone orange and purple. I loved the two-tone effect, but decided on mono colours; candy red was too shouty, it didn't need it.

"I didn't have any inner door skins, so I cut the inner skins out of two rusty Mini doors and welded them to the Cord frames, which gave me inner door handles and window winders. A local engineering shop changed the splines on the winders so I could use the original Cord handles, and the same guys made the outer handles, which are 14" long and designed to look like they're flowing at speed.

"I got it to this stage by Christmas, 2005, so it had gone from a ruin to rolling tub inside two years. The engine is a 305 Chevy, fitted by myself and Dave Harries, who took the trip down several weekends running to work on it with me. I've known Dave for 35 years; he's a very clever man. After Dave got busy at his end, Paul Burnham took over finishing the mechanicals, fitting the air ride and building the engine, and it came back a driver. Martin Bartlett, my friend and ace engineer, took the car and prepped it for paint. He had it for a year! But it's thanks to his patience that I have those 4mm panel gaps all round. He's also the guy that fitted the hideaway headlamps on MX5 actuators. Colin Ware sprayed the two-tone Fiat Abarth colours.

"By this time my head was out of my cars. I had lost interest altogether in the Cord, and if someone had offered to take it off me, I'd have sold it. I'd even applied for planning permission to convert my garages into a house, but this was refused, which is really lucky as my passion has since been reignited! I then met a guy named Andy Barton, who said 'I've heard a rumour that you'd like someone to help you finish the Cord…' A couple of months later, he phoned back and said 'I've handed in my notice; are you still interested?'! He came over and got it running and braking again after many years, and ended up staying to help me get it to the Supernats.

"I decided I wanted to debut the car at the NSRA Supernationals, as that's where I'd taken it back in 2003 with 'Andy Saunders' Next Project' written on it. I had made the front wings and valance into a one-piece nose cone that had been tacked together on the car and then bolted to a purpose-built jig, where it had been since 2009. Six weeks before the Supernats, we unbolted it and attempted to fit it to the car - it fitted, and so did the bonnet, but the grille didn't fit at all. Six weeks before its launch, I ended up rushing to finish a car that had been 14 years in the build. In that last six weeks I was also introduced to a panel beater/artist called Matt who made all of the chrome trims. I'd decided I needed something between the two colours, and

OIL
PRESSURE
SPEED IN MILES
PER HOUR
B0705

LIGHTS
GAS
CHOKE
INST

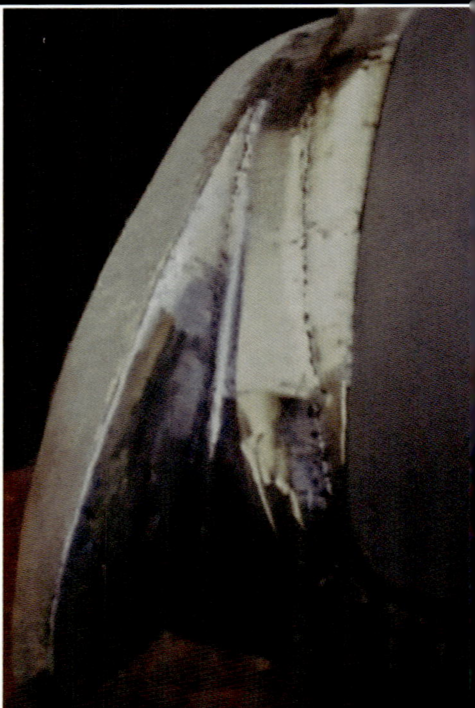

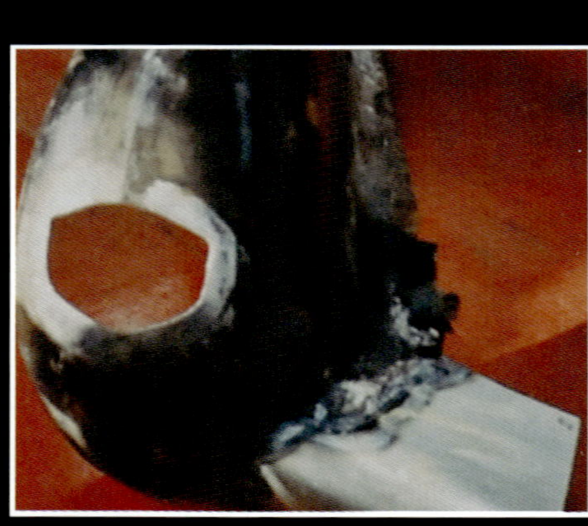
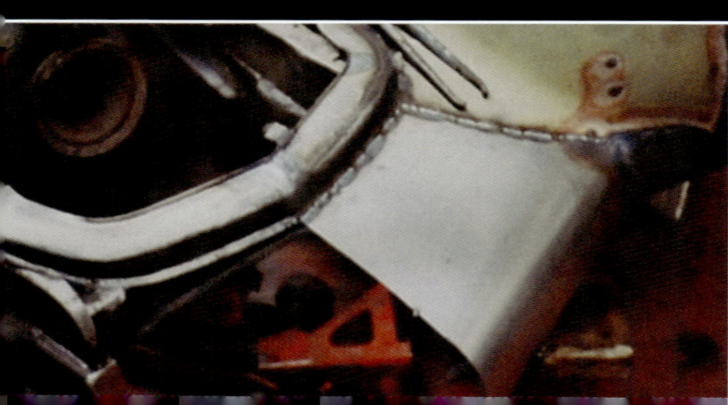

was going to ask Neil Melliard to paint me a divider, but then Matt made me the sweepspears, the screen divider and the boot trim, all out of brass!

"The front seat uses the original steel frame, and is made like buckets although it's a bench. I've no idea what the steering wheel came from although it's definitely German. I got it from Beaulieu Autojumble, and sprayed it to match the interior. I got the wheel centre mirror compact while Christmas shopping in London, and it looks like it was pressed to fit. The scarabs on the seat backs are crystal quartz in a gold surround, lit with LEDs. I used to go to Glastonbury a lot, and was in a shop called Stone Age when I saw some bracelets with these scarabs on. I'd stared at them for 15 minutes before the shopkeeper came and asked if I was alright! I asked him if he could make me two with clasps on the back – Egyptology was a big influence in Art Deco cars."

"Scott Lloyd trimmed the interior, and he's brilliant. When he was still at school he worked with me and finished the 'Incantation' Pontiac for me when my Dad was taken ill. He knew exactly what I wanted on the Cord when I said I want diamond pleat but in an art deco style."

"The dashboard dials are art in themselves. They have the face, then the flat glass with engraved numbers and a green painted edge that, when lit, makes the numbers float above the face, all covered by a domed glass. The steering column was from an early Thunderbird, bought from Angel Autos in Dorchester when he was selling up, that I had rechromed. The switchgear on the dash is original, but had Mazak knobs that were horrible and wouldn't rechrome. I found these diamante knobs that I'd bought from Essen for the Bentley back in about 2000 and never used, so I glued those on, but the switches don't work – all the switches are underneath.

"I knew I wanted the name Tetanus somewhere in the interior, and one day I was at a craft village called Walford Mills, where I saw a lady doing embroidery. Her work was really good, so I asked 'Could you embroider the word Tetanus on a door panel?'! I told her the story of how I found the car all overgrown, and she added the ivy trailing across the word.

"The roll cage around the engine stemmed from an idea Scott mentioned one day about a Maserati birdcage. I kinda styled it on this idea, but in much heavier tube as though to give a nod to its potential heritage of being a stock car."

"I am still getting used to driving her, as the seat is so low that when you're sat in it, the most forward point of the front you see is the inside of the chrome screen surround. I've not taken it far yet, I've only done maybe 70 miles so far, but I'm always nervous driving one of my builds for the first time. It'll only go to shows because it's just too awkward, bulky and flash to cruise and park. For the debut, I liaised with Pike, and it was his idea to unveil it from a trailer. We'd been told that there were only about 10 people waiting, but when the time came to unload it, there were crowds. I was just relieved that it started, but after that, everything was a blur. I stood in the same spot until mid-afternoon, and had so many compliments. A dozen people told me that I'd raised the kustom bar by several pegs, and one Belgian guy said 'You must retire now, because you can never beat this.' Oh, I will…"

Thanks to:

Gary Hawkins way back in 2003 for help in dissembling
Dave Harries, chassis work and suspension
Burnham Autos, engine building, air ride and mechanical finishing
The late Ron Dean, for panel beating
Martin Bartlett, body detailing
Colin Ware, body tub spraying
John Bethall, front end spraying
Auburn Cord Duesenberg Parts, Kansas, for Cord parts
Scott Lloyd, trimming
Jen Goodwin, embroidery
Dave Hayward, detailed parts.
Mat Edley (The Dorset Copperfish), for chrome trims
Andy Barton, help in finishing and relighting my passion for building cars
Approximately 7,000 hours went into the build of this car.

Words: Dave Smith
Photos: Matt Woods & Larry O'Toole

Photos: Larry & Al O'Toole

CASTLEMAINE, AUSTRALIA

Few hot rodding publications can boast an uninterrupted history of 40 years but Australian Street Rodding reached that milestone in March 2017. To celebrate, a function was held at the Old Castlemaine Gaol the weekend before the ASRF Street Rod Nationals in Bendigo.

This gave interstate rodders an opportunity to add it to their travel plans for the Nationals, so there were attendees from all Australian states amongst the crowd. Speeches were short and a few prizes were given out to selected car owners, plus presentations made to the four original partners in the business, all of whom still live in Castlemaine. ■

RIGHT: The parking area outside the Old Castlemaine Gaol was filled to capacity with visiting rods from all over Australia. The satin black '34 Ford three window coupe runs a small block Ford, next is Ian Hickey's '37 Ford pickup with '35 grille, the silver '34 Ford three window coupe belongs to Claude Pesce from WA and the gold channelled '34 Ford coupe is owned by Bruce Rhue from Kilmore.

MAIN: The display of rods and customs inside the Old Castlemaine Gaol wall was just as impressive as those outside. In the foreground is Geoff Knape's orange '34 Ford Tudor, the satin black '32 Ford five window coupe belongs to John Philpot from northern New South Wales and the green '32 Ford Tudor is Kathleen Alldrick's cool family car.

ABOVE: There have been a lot of other publications other than Australian Street Rodding produced over the 40 years, many of which were featured in this extensive display.

ABOVE RIGHT: The four original partners that started Graffiti Publications. From left to right they are Brian Bannerman, Colin Hall, Geoff Knape and Larry O'Toole. All are still living in Castlemaine.

ABOVE: The Old Castlemaine Gaol provided the perfect backdrop for the 40th celebrations. Outside the rear gate of the gaol is the stock looking but potent big block Ford powered Model A coupe of Shaun Colliver with a '34 Ford coupe rolling by in the background.

LEFT: Retired art teacher, John Holland designed the Graffiti logo back in 1977 and it is still in use today. John was on hand to sign his original artwork that was drawn on a scrap of paper all those years ago.

BELOW: The Graffiti fleet. Left to right they are the recently completed '36 Ford Tudor project car, the '30 Model A pickup (also a project car) that was completed in 1990, the '28 Model A Tudor (Custom Rodder project car) that has been on the road since 1976 and XP 1000 Falcon sedan delivery that was first completed in 1982 and rebuilt twice since. The Willys tourer on the end belongs to ASR Tech Workshop column editor, Ted Robinette.

ABOVE: Rodders who accepted our open invite enjoyed a fantastic day of reminiscing, catching up with old friends and meeting new friends. For many it was an opportunity to meet people whose names they knew but had never met in person.

RIGHT: Three of the attending rods were selected by family members as their choice for the day. Here Glen Anderson from Western Australia receives a 40th Anniversary banner from Al O'Toole as a prize for his candy apple red '34 Ford coupe.

LEFT: Larry, Mary and Al O'Toole cut the 40th Anniversary cake that was then shared among all the attendees.

RIGHT: Everyone signed a 40th Anniversary banner as they entered the venue and it now hangs in our office.

BELOW: Here's another view of the Graffiti fleet of rods and customs together with Tech Workshop editor, Ted Robinette's rare '40 Willys tourer.

ABOVE: Participants visited the Castlemaine Hot Rod Centre hosted "Kulture", automotive art show at The Mill complex.

ABOVE RIGHT: This pair automatically had priority parking rights out the front of the Theatre Royal where American Graffiti screened.

MAIN: Chris Maxwell's Model A coupe, Larry O'Toole's '36 Ford Tudor and Ian Hickey's '37 Ford pickup set the mood.

To cater for the extensive numbers of street rodders travelling to Bendigo in central Victoria for the ASRF Street Rod Nationals, Castlemaine Rods decided to host a Pre-Nationals Rod Run in their near-by township to give early arrivals another event to enjoy.

The Pre-Nationals Run took place on the Wednesday immediately preceding Easter. Many of the participants were from interstate, having turned their trip to the Nationals into a vacation and keen to see as much of the local area as possible.

The Participants of the Pre-Nationals Run assembled at Hadfield's Hot Rods on the outskirts of Castlemaine and travelled from there into the city itself via a scenic route, with a shop visit to CAE Performance, and ended at The Mill with its host of tourist activities to enjoy. Those keen to do so were guided to a horse-drawn carriage museum as well, and the run concluded with dinner and a movie at the historic Theatre Royal. ■

ABOVE: Chopped Aussie bodied '34 Ford coupe of Peter Simmonds from Gosnells, Western Australia was one of many interstate rodders enjoying their time in central Victoria prior to the ASRF Street Rod Nationals.

LEFT: Ray Charlton's delightful '48 Ford convertible mixes comfort with style perfectly. Under the bonnet is a 351 Windsor and the ride is nice thanks to A Jaguar independent front end. There's a full feature on this and Ray's Deuce coupe starting on page 162 of this issue of Hot Rodding International.

BELOW: There's always another project car for Aussie Desert Cooler man Norm Hardinge and this time it's this hiboy '32 Ford roadster that was on display inside Hadfield's Hot Rods during the Pre-Nationals Run.

BELOW: Adam Birch entered the Pre-Nationals Run in his recently acquired '61 Ford Ranch Wagon with irridescent green paint and white highlights. Adam is a member of the host club Castlemaine Rods.

BOTTOM: Rods and customs assembled at Hadfield's Hot Rods for the start of the Pre-Nationals Run where they enjoyed morning tea before setting off on a cruise around the central Victorian township which is the self-proclaimed Street Rod Centre of Australia.

LEFT: Glen Anderson leads this group on the cruise around Castlemaine in his brilliant candy-apple red '34 Ford coupe from Western Australia.
BELOW: The late Bill Mussett's superb Deuce three window coupe was on display while at Hadfield's Hot Rods prior to the start of the cruise.

ABOVE: Tony Steiner's '39 Ford is an improved restoration that gets into the rodding mood with scallops at the fender openings.
MAIN: Patrons were able to tour the museum at Hadfield's Hot Rods while enjoying morning tea before the cruise around Castlemaine began.

ABOVE: Satin black and beastly looking '40 Ford pickup has blown Chevy engine, chopped top and big diameter wheels with low profile tyres. Owner is Peter Ellis.

BELOW: The scene outside the Theatre Royal where entrants enjoyed a kebab dinner prior to the screening of the movie American Graffiti. In the foreground is Con Soldatos' LS Chevy powered HG Holden panel van with Monaro front panels.

BOTTOM: What better place to witness the streets crawling with rods and customs than the streets of Castlemaine on the Wednesday prior to the ASRF Street Rod Nationals in nearby Bendigo?

TOP: Local drag racer and hot rodder Chris Soldatos has another street rod project under way, this '32 Ford hiboy roadster that was sitting in his brother Con's CAE Performance workshop. Chris also owns one of Australia's top Pro-Stock racers.

ABOVE: Part of the "Kulture" art show at The Mill was this display of local artist, Stuart Spragg's corrugated iron artwork.

ABOVE: Two Western Australian rods share the parking area outside CAE Performance during the Pre-Nationals Run. In the lead is Chris Maxwell's '30 Model A Ford coupe with '28 grille. Behind is Les Moran's immaculate flathead powered '32 Ford five window coupe.

BELOW: It's hard to resist a photo of two hiboys in their element — on the road. In front is the bare metal '32 Ford of Marcel Berkhout with Julie Loomes' red Model A following behind.

BOTTOM: Two way traffic during the cruise around town has rods and customs passing each other and creating a spectacle for all to enjoy.

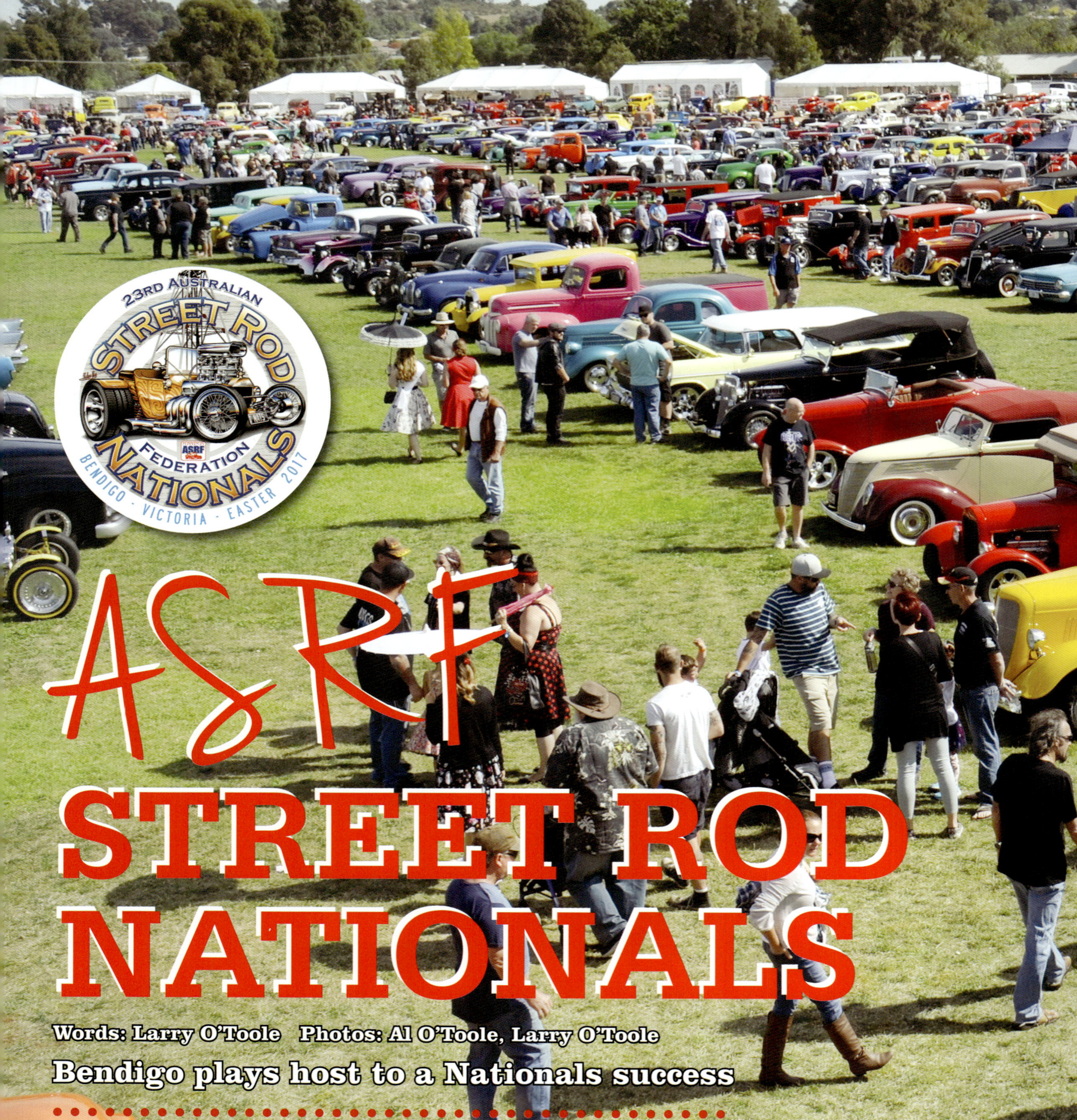

ASRF STREET ROD NATIONALS

Words: Larry O'Toole   Photos: Al O'Toole, Larry O'Toole

Bendigo plays host to a Nationals success

Bendigo hosted the 23rd ASRF Nationals over Easter 2017 and many declared the event to be a resounding success, and for good reason. Records were broken, good times were had and the weather couldn't have been better. The Prince of Wales Showgrounds was packed to capacity with campers and cool cars for four days and thousands of people came to get a look at some of the best street rods from all over Australia.

Friday was "entrants only day" featuring the massive traders hall, cruising the showgrounds, a scale model and memorabilia display, trolley challenge, mini rods, themed drive-by judging, dyno shootout competition and the driving events – Bag of Gold Drop and Go-Whoa. The live band, Itchy Fingers followed a sausage sizzle and the official opening of the event while cruising around the showgrounds outside continued until 10:00pm.

On Saturday, the Nationals was open to the public and the front gates were overwhelmed with keen punters lined up for hundreds of metres to get into the Prince of Wales Showgrounds to see the largest ever Street Rod Nationals! Over 10,000 people poured through the gates

and enjoyed the record number of entries, nearly 1400 in total!

Entrants voted for their favourite cars during the show and shine and took in all the same events that the Friday offered, plus a spark plug racing competition, a ladies afternoon tea featuring drinks, nibbles and a fashion show and an evening dinner followed by the Wendy Stapleton Paul Norton Band.

Easter Sunday was another busy day starting with breakfast for entrants, a chapel service hosted by the Christian Rodders and another full itinerary of activities to occupy both entrants and visitors. Even the Easter Bunny made an appearance. The Go-Whoa finals started after lunch with a large field of entries narrowed down to the rodders with the fastest times left to battle for the crown. The much-anticipated drawing of the ASRF raffle car took place late in the afternoon, followed by auctions, presentations and another live band, Cool Change rounding out the evening and bringing one of the best Nationals ever to a close.

ABOVE: Bright green '34 Ford three window coupe of Peter Raines cruises past Colin Manglesdorf's '36 Ford Cabriolet and wife, Jan Manglesdorf's equally immaculate '36 Ford pickup.

RIGHT: Heading this line up of rods cruising around the main oval is Laine Engellenner's hiboy '34 Ford three window coupe followed by Ronald McKenna's Deuce five window coupe.

BELOW RIGHT: Hand built roadsters don't come any finer than Mick Renfrey's sleek '33 Ford version that he built himself over an extended period. It was one of the Top Twenty cars at the Nationals.

BELOW: Display of historic hot rods and paraphenalia inside the main building included Leo Spessot's flamed '40 Ford convertible, Eddie Ford's silver '32 Ford three window coupe and the SA Rod & Custom Club's Dodge C-cab truck.

RIGHT: Originally built by McDonald Bros many years ago, this blown Buick Nailhead powered T bucket is now in the hands of Karl Gunther.

TOP LEFT: You don't often see '36 Chevy tourers as street rods and there is none better than Glenn Whittingham's gold example that was built by his late father.

TOP RIGHT: All the way from Port Lincoln were Mark and Terisa Paynter in Terisa's superb '37 Chevy sedan that has been in the family for many years. Recently rebuilt as a street rod it has LS1 Chevy running gear from a VZ Holden HDT ute.

ABOVE: Popular winner of the Top Street Rod award was Mick Speranza with his immaculate '35 Ford coupe. The chopped black beauty is 350 Chevy powered and rides on Halibrand wheels.

LEFT: Mick Speranza shares the limelight with the other Top Twenty trophy winners at the conclusion of the presentations.

TOP LEFT: Truly a street gasser is this flip front, blown Hemi powered purple '41 Willys coupe owned by Peter Lyons.

TOP RIGHT: The Easter Bunny is always a highlight of the Nationals for the kids. It's always the same prominent Australian hot rodder sweltering inside that suit.

ABOVE: Blown Ardun power attracts your attention to Roger Brockway's blue channelled '34 Ford coupe immediately. Beside it is the green and white '54 Chevy two door sedan of Jason Bell.

LEFT: Straight, black and perfect sums up the beautiful '41 Ford pickup of Neil Ide from south coast NSW.

BELOW: Malcolm Mountjoy won the first ASRF raffle car T bucket and he has owned and maintained it ever since.

TOP LEFT: All the correct period speed equipment appears on the flathead engine in Leslie Ireland's '27 Dodge bucket.
TOP RIGHT: Simon and Di Cunningham's all steel '37 Ford cabriolet is entirely owner built and driven from Tasmania for the Nationals.
ABOVE: Pair of nicely turned out Model A Fords are Mark Donnellan's irridescent red '31 model on the left and Garry Ritchie's purple '29 model on the right. Both are members of Castlemaine Rods.
LEFT: There was lots of sheet metal to get straight before painting black on Ben Walker's '48 Chrysler coupe from Tasmania. Under the bonnet is a late model 5.7 Hemi engine.

ABOVE: South Australian rodder Phil Air owns the purple '31 Model A hiboy that sits beside Denis Carolan's magenta '48 Mercury sedan.
LEFT: Looking resplendent in cherry paint is Vicki Munday's classy '56 Ford Victoria that is 5.0 injected Ford powered.
BELOW: Alan Shuttleworth used a classic old Peterbilt truck to carry his light green '46 GMC pickup down from NSW for the Nationals.

TOP LEFT: Corey Wilson inherited his late father's '42 Ford coupe, got it back together and running again and was rewarded with the encouragement award at the Nationals. Behind is Geoff Knape's '34 Ford roadster with Robert Wilson's green '35 Ford coupe.

TOP RIGHT: Andy Reid swapped shiny wheels for painted wires on his immaculate '36 Ford three window coupe.

ABOVE: Graeme Martin brought his swoopy Ford single spinner convertible over from Tasmania and wowed the large and appreciative crowd. The wild two tone purple convertible was built from the remains of a sedan.

BELOW: Richard Watkins did a sterling job of creating his phantom '34 Ford cabriolet pickup.

ASRF SR NATS

ABOVE: The junior rodders had their own dedicated cruising track where they could drive the mini rods all day long in safety.
LEFT: Jason Taranto's '58 star model Ford Mainline ute is typical of the family's collection of neat mid-fifties Fords.

RIGHT: Ramp truck and pickup combination belongs to Robert Rawlings from Chisholm in the ACT. The truck is a '41 Chevy cab-over while the pickup is a '46 Chevy long bed with chopped top and custom headlight treatment.
BELOW: The superb blue '32 Ford five window coupe is Les Moran's from WA parked alongside Ken Taig's equally nice '32 Ford Victoria from the local Bendigo area.
BELOW RIGHT: Outstanding '49 Ford woody with nothing less than Huon pine inserts is the handiwork of John Viles from Central Coast NSW. It's Ford powered.

RIGHT: If there are driving events to take part in, Neil Davis will be there in his yellow Model A roadster. Lots of rodders entered the Go-Whoa competition held within the showgrounds complex in a dedicated area.

RIGHT: Bare metal Deuce hiboy roadster with American Racing Wheels five spokes and small block Chevy engine is owned by Marcel Berkhout from the appropriately named Byford, WA.

ABOVE: You won't find a tidier early Falcon wagon than Craig Mansfield's bronze and white '63 XL version that runs late model injected 302 Ford powerplant.

RIGHT: What a great sense of style is portrayed by Steve Walsh's chopped '36 Ford three window coupe that rolls on whitewall shod Kelsey Hayes wire wheels and has black and red tuck and roll interior trim.

BELOW: Why not bring along the vintage motorcycle too? That's what Geoff Weigand did in the bed of his '33 Ford closed cab pickup from the Bay Area Hot Rod Club in Sydney.

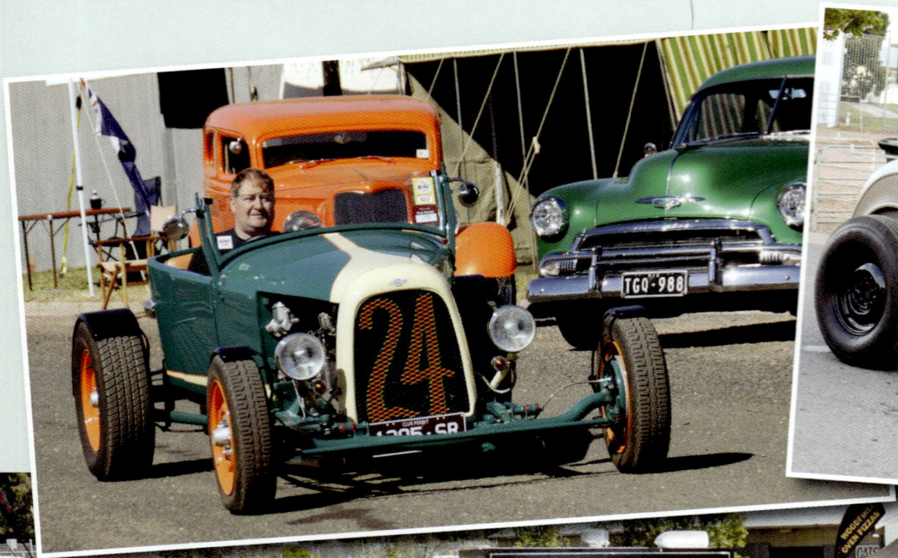

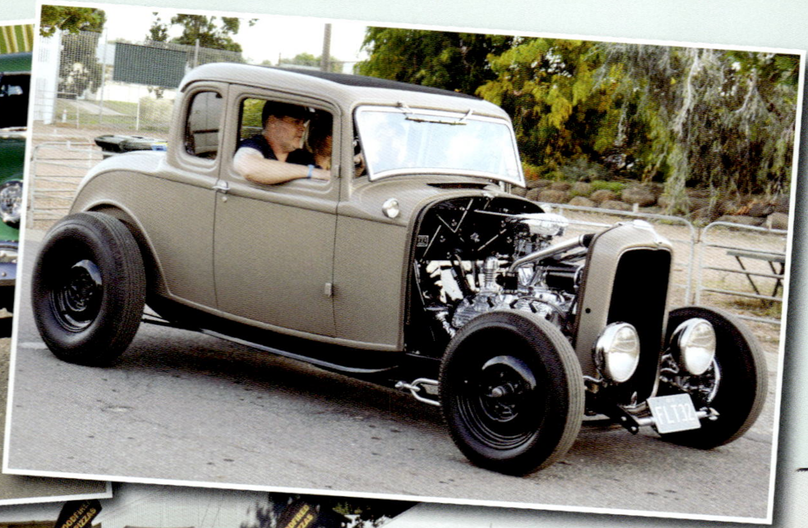

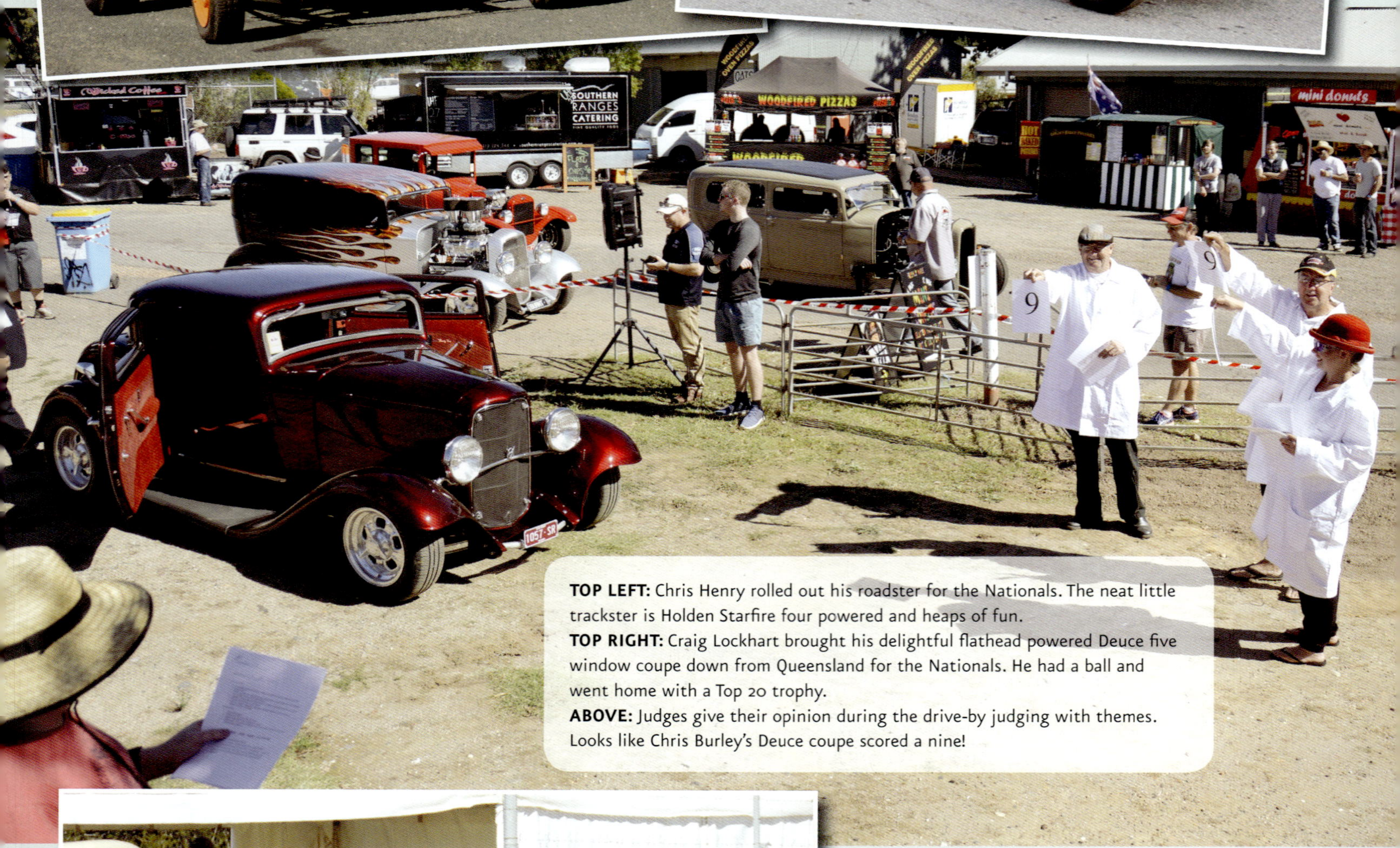

TOP LEFT: Chris Henry rolled out his roadster for the Nationals. The neat little trackster is Holden Starfire four powered and heaps of fun.
TOP RIGHT: Craig Lockhart brought his delightful flathead powered Deuce five window coupe down from Queensland for the Nationals. He had a ball and went home with a Top 20 trophy.
ABOVE: Judges give their opinion during the drive-by judging with themes. Looks like Chris Burley's Deuce coupe scored a nine!

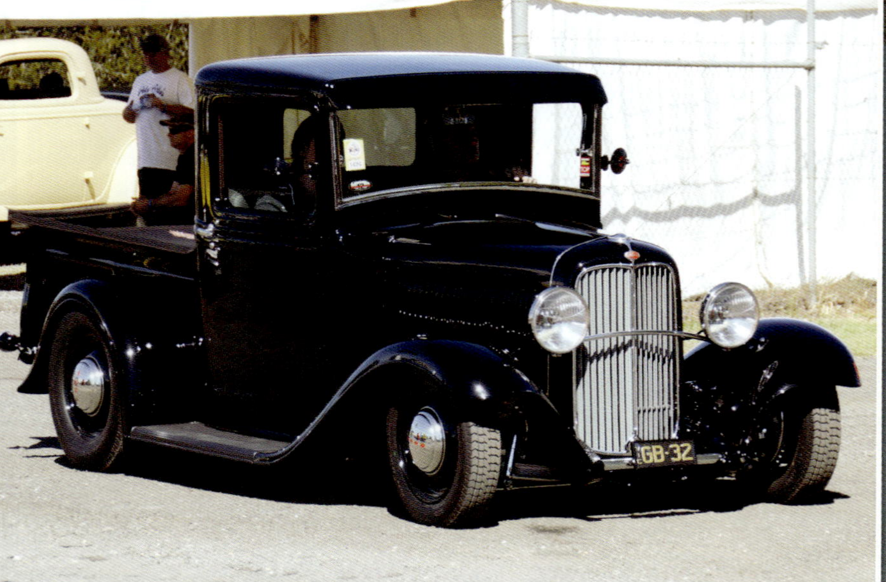

LEFT: Superb is the only way to describe Gary Brown's '32 Ford pickup with Pines Winterfront grille and perfect black paint.
BELOW: Even the little guys take the go-whoa seriously. This competitor has made a perfect stop right on the line.

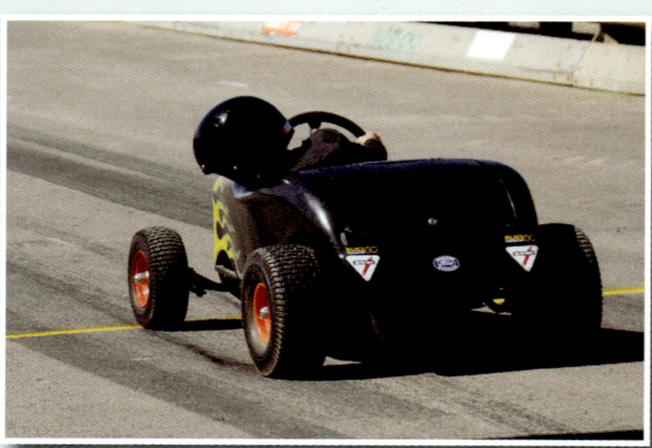

TOP LEFT & INSET: There's a lot of plumbing in the engine bay of Ray Hutchen's quad turbocharged Jaguar V12 '27 Chrysler roadster.

TOP RIGHT: The Henry J is Joanne Fregon's latest project, sharing space with Ian Eliason's '34 Ford coupe on the Lilow Auto Tech stand.

MAIN PIC: David Murphy's spectacular '32 Ford roadster was an outstanding attraction in the trade stand building. It's Y block powered, has brown interior trim and was built to perfection by Deluxe Hot Rod Shop.

ABOVE: Junior entrants stop by the Graffiti Publications trade stand to persue a challenge of the kids scavenger hunt.

LEFT: Our own Project '36 Ford Tudor sat beside our trade stand on Friday where Nationals visitors had the first opportunity to see it up close. Club Permit plates went on just one week prior to the Nationals.

ABOVE: Pure hot rod is the only way to describe Tony Jenkins' Deuce Tudor with chopped top and Nailhead Buick engine.
ABOVE LEFT: Len Souter's '27 T roadster has a Westcott fibreglass repro body painted Toreador Red metallic with tan leather interior. The engine is a '33 C model four banger with a Riley Price overhead valve conversion backed with a '39 Ford gearbox.
ABOVE: Bright red paint, whitewall tyres and a just right rake adds up to a super '33 Ford coupe owned by Chris Dansie.
LEFT: Another four banger equipped rod with overhead valve conversion, this time Alan Hale's Top 20 trophy winning Model A Tudor that has details galore and a black and white theme carried out to perfection.

ASRF 23RD STREET ROD NATIONALS TROPHY WINNERS

Mini Rods

Top Cruiser	Toby Adams
Top Mini Rod	Zach Hughes

Model Cars

Top Adult Model	Colin Farnham
Top Junior Model	Evan
Top Modified Model	Jordan Grech
Top Display Model	Tony Steiner

Bag of Gold Drop

Top Eliminator	Jack McClelland
Best of the Rest	Andrew Hall

Drive-By Judging

Andrew & Lynda Eleftheriou, Gangster themed 1928 Dodge

Trolley Challenge

Winner	Thomas Bath and Cameron Maher
Best of the Rest	Grace Maher and Emily Bath

Spark Plug Racing

First	Bill Duyvestyn
Second	John Burney

Dyno Challenge

Top Six Cylinder Blown	Aaron Cole
Top Six Cylinder N/A	Matt Steele
Top Blown	Wayne Sampson
Top Naturally Aspirated	William Hill

Go Whoa

Ladies Winner	Kim Bevan
Gents Winner	Wayne Sampson

Longest Distance Driven

Tony Brittain, 1947 Ford Pickup, Bunbury, WA

Hard Luck

Bob Ellis, 1941 Willys coupe

Encouragement Award

Corey Wilson, 1942 Ford coupe

Top Represented Victorian Club

Geelong Street Rodders, 39 Entrants

Top Represented Interstate Club

Romans Hot Rod Association, 22 Entrants

Top 20

1. Neale Ide, 1941 Ford pickup
2. Syl Zammit, 1948 Ford panel delivery
3. Alan Hale, 1928 Ford Tudor
4. Tony Murray, 1948 Chev COE
5. Michael Renfrey, 1933 Ford roadster
6. Neville Haynes, 1941 Willys coupe
7. Graeme Martin, 1949 Ford Single Spinner
8. Gunter Maric, 1935 Ford pickup
9. Gary Brown, 1932 Ford pickup
10. Chad Murray, 1933 Ford Victoria
11. Michael Speranza, 1935 Ford coupe
12. Greg Jones, 1935 Ford pickup
13. Ray Pearman, 1956 Buick hardtop
14. Michael Kibblewhite, 1951 Chev ute
15. John Viles, 1949 Ford woody
16. Robert Dickson, 1950 Mercury coupe
17. Scott Marshall, 1941 Willys coupe
18. Craig Lockhart, 1932 Ford coupe
19. Robert Rawlings, 1941 Chev COE
20. Andrew Reid, 1936 Ford coupe

Top Car Winner

Michael Speranza, 1935 Ford coupe

ABOVE: An unusual combination of old '46 Morris truck parts and a custom made bed results in a neat and inexpensive street rod for owner Robert Stocks.

LEFT: Straight black '35 Ford pickup owned by Gunter Maric is a delight to the eye and was a Top 20 trophy winner.

BELOW: Authentic looking '41 Willys coupe gasser of Robert Monea has the correct stance and original Halibrand Magnesium wheels.

ABOVE LEFT: Top class Mercury lead sled custom of Robert Dickson has all of the right appointments including lakes pipes, heavy roof chop, custom grille and superb paintwork. Another Top 20 trophy winner.

ABOVE: Lighting up the go-whoa track is Ross Mayes in his chopped and flamed '32 Ford Tudor that features big block Chevy powerplant and independent front suspension.

KOOL 30

The Real Thing
NEW ZEALAND

Jack Martin & Louise Smith's 1930 Model A Coupe

- **Jack Martin & Louise Smith**
- **1930 Model A Ford Coupe**
- **Southern City Cruisers**
- **Auckland, New Zealand**

Words: Greg Stokes
Photos: Greg Stokes

We've always said history has a strange way of repeating itself and there are numerous aspects to the Model A coupe you see here that reflect upon its owner's history in hot rodding. This car is also one of those that hit the scene and you are immediately taken by its beauty or perfection – you look at it, smile and say "Oh yeah, it's got the look!"

Jack Martin and Louise Smith have good reason to smile as their freshly built hot rod ticks all the boxes in terms of stance, style, proportion and finish. Appropriately named "KOOL 30", Jack and Louise's 1930 Ford Model A coupe is rather different to when it first rolled off the production line at Ford Motor Company. The sparkling GM Synergy Green metallic all-steel bodied hot rod is the perfect stablemate to their well-travelled, red 1928 Ford Model A A-400. The couple are members of the South City Cruisers that is a family orientated hot rod club catering for members with hot rod and custom vehicles very much like "KOOL 30".

Jack first started hot rodding in the seventies while working at Auckland's Greenlane Speed Shop and built a show winning Ford Model T-bucket that featured on the cover of the New Zealand Hot Rod magazine. This car is still around to this day, looking similar to when Jack built it, that is testament to his talent and ability. In the eighties he built a well detailed and finished, bright yellow 1933 Ford four-door sedan that was featured in Australian Street Rodding magazine. Like the former T-bucket, the sedan has also stood the test of time, living in the Taranaki area today, but repainted in bright red. After the sedan, Jack took a break from hot rodding and concentrated on building mostly plastic and a few die-cast kit set model cars with incredible detail. To say he got into it seriously was an understatement, producing a full range of resin parts for himself and other modellers. Together with fellow model car builders Bruce Swallow and Mike Pringle, among others, MPH "Miniature Petrol Heads" was formed. The club is still going and Jack hasn't lost touch with the smaller scale of rodding he enjoyed, but in more recent times he's found himself wanting to build another full-size hot rod.

Childhood inspiration from a Model A Ford coupe led to the decision to build a traditional styled version on a 1932 Ford frame in hiboy style. The choice of the 283 cubic inch Chevrolet V8 engine with four Stromberg 97 carburettors on an Offenhauser intake manifold with chrome megaphone headers out the sides fits with that traditional style.

In 2009 a parts car was imported from the USA that started Jack on the journey of the childhood dream becoming a reality. This gave him the original Ford all steel body and shortly thereafter other parts were accumulated, including the engine and a bare 1932 Ford chassis. They served as the foundation for the project. He tinkered away in the garage at home making brackets and mounting suspension pieces and drive train before calling upon Graeme and Greg at Mac's Speed Shop in Whitford, East

www.graffitipub.com.au

Auckland to help hurry things along. Meanwhile, Simon Tippens at Creative Metal Works in Pukekohe had been working away on the body and fitting new patch panels as well as carrying out the roof chop, plus a few other hot rod body modifications.

Then the body was sent to Mac's Speed Shop to be fitted up to the completed chassis. Other modifications were carried out by Graeme and Greg at Mac's to ensure the car was built to New Zealand's modified vehicle standards and regulations that were all signed off by Mark Stokes at MS Vehicle Certification. The body was then finally prepared for paint by Scott Tercel before Johnny Antonievich and Mike Lee at Antonievich Restorations further prepared all the body and components for the electrifying GM Synergy Green paint. The coupe was fully assembled at Mac's Speed Shop and test driven before being sent to Shawn Horwood at Action Canvas & Upholstery at Mount Maunganui. Louise provided invaluable input after being labelled as "Jan Beck – The Colour Consultant" by Graeme at Mac's Speed Shop. When Jack was doing the dance as to what colour to paint the car it was Louise who kept things in line and offered a woman's perspective to reassure Jack of his original vision. It was Louise who perused the colour swatches at the upholstery shop, selecting the cream shade called Merino leather that contrasts perfectly against the green, the chrome and the polished aluminium.

While the coupe has been finished to an immaculate standard, Jack and Louise strongly believe in driving their cars and already it's hard to get them to stand still with this one. Who can blame them really? KOOL 30 is comfortable to ride in and easy to drive and it cuts a cool profile going down the road. At its first event in early March 2017, KOOL 30 picked up Manager's Choice at the Bellagio Petrolhead Breakfast in Manukau City and then later that day at the Manukau Rod & Custom Club Rod Run it was awarded Top Five Car. Later in the year it was awarded second place in the Custom Hot Rod Coupe Class at the Teng Tools Grand National Rod & Custom Show and then at the NZHRA Street Rod Nationals in Palmerston North, the cool lil' coupe was awarded a Top Ten Place and Best Traditional Hot Rod Awards. But it's not about prizes for Jack and Louise, it's all about having fun with cars with their fellow South City Cruisers members and other hot rodders all over New Zealand.

7th Annual Tucson Dragway Reunion

"Build it and they will come"

Story: Bob Honeybrook Photos: Mike Bieke

ABOVE: Aussies Ross and Jude Preen had their "Banshee" fueler on hand for the event with flag proudly flying off the rear of the blown Hemi powered dragster.

Dan Owens, Walter Nash, Red Greth and Paula Roth put their money where their mouths were to build the Tucson Dragway Reunion into a viable show that has improved and gained creedence over the past seven years.

The feedback I had received from people who had attended influenced me to make the trip from Sydney, Australia to Tucson, Arizona to check out the action that was on hand. I travelled to Los Angeles on the same flight as Ross and Jude Preen who were going to the US to do the Tucson Dragway Reunion and then bring their AA/FD "Banshee" back home to Australia. We made our connecting flight from Los Angeles to Phoenix, Arizona where Ross and Jude were to pick up the "Banshee". I collected my Chrysler 300 and located my motel, only getting lost twice. I also picked up a flu type bug that laid me low for a couple of days. Wednesday evening I showed my DVD of the 1966 US Drag Fest in Australia to a group of racers at Paula Roth's place. Thursday morning I made the drive from Phoenix to Tucson and met up with Australian Hot Rodder Paul Northey at the motel where a large number of the friendly participants were staying. The Kick Off Party at the Cell Trees Race Shop commenced at 3:00pm. The three ingredients were friends, food and nitro race cars and they made a great dish to enjoy during the night while making new friends and renewing some old acquaintances. This event is endorsed by the internet based 1320 Group which is a group of historic racers that are dedicated to preserving the history of the sport of Drag Racing. Sponsors for this event include Good Vibrations Motorsports, Cell Trees Race Shop, Merles Auto Parts and Unified Services.

The Grand Marshall of the event was Steve Gibbs, supported by special guests Doug Thorley of Doug's Headers. "The Hawaiian" Roland Leong, John Dearmore, David Pace, Announcer Bruce Mabry with Jon Lundberg as Special Announcer.

Over thirty Fuel Cars and a similar number of Classic Gassers, plus some Exhibition Cars attended. Additionally there were thirty-five Show Cars. For the Altered fans there were thirteen Fuel Altereds to entertain the crowd. This event shares the track with the Western Fuel Altereds, who run a Chicago style event. In addition there was a bracket for Pre 1989 cars that was sponsored by the track owner, and another

TOP LEFT & RIGHT: Slingshot dragster of Paula Roth who helped stage the drags and the flamed Pontiac GTO funny car of Tony Ribeau, driver Trevor Laron.
ABOVE LEFT: The "Li'l Ol' Whine Maker" is a rear engine early funny car based on a Dodge Dart that is owned by Ed Phillips and driven by Eddie Paulson. The car was built and raced in the sixties by same pair.
ABOVE RIGHT: Street rods and custom cars get to park in their own secure area and provide patrons with an extra car show as part of the reunion.

MAIN: The Seevers/Wiesner/Owens A/Gas Supercharged Oldsmobile powered '37 Willys was a standout. It was campaigned from 1962-1966. This tribute version was put together by team member Del Wiesner.

ABOVE: The Green Monster featured dual slicks on the rear and a monstrous V12 Allison powerplant.

ABOVE: Doug Thorley poses with the reproduction version of his "Doug's Headers" Corvair funny car owned by Paul Brown. Doug was coaxed into the driver's seat of the car for its initial fire-up that really impressed the crowd.

thirty show cars were on display in the area set aside for these neat machines. This event is organised to attract all of the historic style cars and the people that enjoy viewing them, along with meeting the crewmen, drivers, photographers/media, track workers and all who helped to make up the history of the sport. We made it to the track early on Friday and wandered the pits checking out the fine variety of race cars that were steadily arriving and setting up to take part in the show. The track was hot from 6:00pm to 10:00pm for cars running the pre '89 Bracket, along with the vintage race car push starts and cackle cars. The highlight for me was the arrival of the repop of the Roland Leong "Hawaiian". Roland and Suzi were there to view the car. When Roland debuted his "Hawaiian" he crashed the car and destroyed it on the first pass after clocking an 8.01/191mph. The crew with the new dragster did their homework, when the original "Hawaiian" rail was built there were two identical cars built side by side and the second car went to Texas where it had a short life as a race car and it was then stored in the shed after the engine was removed. The rail was recovered, including the engine, and it is now "The Hawaiian". This car is a beauty.

For all that remember the "Doug's Headers" Corvair AA/FC a new repro was on hand to pay tribute to Doug Thorley. Doug and family were there to take part in the unveiling of this fine machine. Doug was coaxed into the seat and it was given a fire-up that impressed the crowd who were there to see the legend, Doug Thorley.

John Dearmore presented his AA/FD that is a sight to behold. This dragster is as neat as any you will ever see. The Dragster top qualified at the 1970 Indianapolis Nationals running a 6.49 et. Dearmore's car was powered by a 392 Hemi overbored .030" making it 398 cubic inches. The best bits of 1969 were fitted to the engine including Mondello cylinder heads, Enderle fuel injection, a Hampton blower and a Hays clutch. Dearmore's 190" wheelbase dragster was constructed by SPE Chassis, fitted with a Tom Hanna body painted by Nat Quick and trimmed by Tony Nancy. This machine was stored away for almost four decades and is now enjoying its share of sunshine.

Among a number of Gassers the Seevers, Wiesner and Owens A/Gas Supercharged Oldsmobile powered machine was a standout. It was campaigned from 1962 to 1966. A 1962 Oldsmobile 394 was taken out to 400 cubic inches, fitted with a 6-71 blower and two port Hilborn injection and it used an automatic transmission. The original trans was a Turbo Hydro four speed, but the car now has a two speed Powerglide and a Ford nine inch rear end. The original machine ran a best of 10.00 at 196mph. This '37 Willys is a fine tribute to the team put together by original team member Dale Wiesner.

The highlights of the event on Friday and Saturday were the vintage race car push starts and the Cackle Cars. What a great show they put on. The Tucson Dragway Reunion is a credit to all involved. This event has been running for seven years now and with quality people at the head it will no doubt improve every year. The organising committee are to be commended for their efforts. ■

ABOVE The Speed-Sport Special of Red Greth looks the part with matching push car. Above right Steve Gibbs with a happy band of supporters after receiving an award for his long service to drag racing.

BELOW: Roland Leong's famous "Hawaiian" dragster, lives again thanks to the fact that an identical dragster was built at the same time and was used for this accurate re-creation.

INSET LEFT: Roland Leong (left) stands proudly with Frank Henig, owner of the "Hawaiian".

ABOVE CLOCKWISE: The Scorpion dragster drips with period correct appointments because it is just that, an original survivor that was stored for decades. Doug Thorley sits in the cockpit of the "Doug's Headers" Corvair Funny Car owned by Paul Brown. Narrow bodied fuel altered of Kevin Knowles warms the tyres. Joe Morrison's blue '34 Ford fuel coupe driven by Ted Brine is a fine looking piece that creates excitement for the fans.

MAIN: Can you taste the atmosphere? Presentations under lights in front of the crowd gives a real sense of appreciation for these nostalgia race cars, just add smoke and fire!

All Roads Lead to Louisville

The 48th Annual NSRA Street Rod Nationals Plus

Words & Photos: Larry O'Toole & Al O'Toole

BELOW: John Martin's incredible '34 Ford coupe boasts an injected 693ci big block Chevy tuned to produce 825 horsepower! The chopped steel body is fitted with a full race cage and features a restyled cowl that is shaped to match the grille.

BELOW RIGHT: Local Louisville hot rodder, Alan Player entered his '33 Ford pickup. The hiboy runs a tri-powered Buick Nailhead V8, finned brakes, a dropped and drilled beam axle and features white tuck and roll interior trim.

OPPOSITE PAGE BELOW LEFT: Harold and Sally Michael from Hamilton, Michigan own this big block motivated '64 Corvette with Billet Specialties wheels and red leather trim. It was one of the Pro's Pick Top 12 winners.

OPPOSITE PAGE BELOW RIGHT: Leo Payne's '31 Ford blends Model A coupe and Tudor styling with McCulloch supercharged flathead power.

Seventeen Aussies joined us for our 2017 NSRA Nationals tour and although some had been to this incredible event before, everyone was blown away with the magnitude of the enormous show.

The integration of the rolling 30 year cut-off date for entrant vehicles has seen an increase of the later model cars at Louisville, but with over 10,000 entries all up, there are still far more cool early hot rods to see than one person can possibly take in over the four day event.

While there aren't too many rodders that choose to debut their cars at this event, it is the ideal chance to get a look at some of the best hot rods from the first half of the year. We noticed that this year there were a lot of high end builds that had been shown at the most prestigious shows in the USA. Entries from the AMBR contest at the Grand National Roadster Show and Ridler Award contenders from the Detroit Autorama were on display throughout the Kentucky Exposition Centre with several high calibre hot rods taking pride of place at vendor booths inside, in the Builder's Showcase area and outside amongst the field of regular entrants.

Aussie rodders Roger and Jenny Vagg had their '32 Ford five window coupe at the Nationals and were overjoyed to be selected in the Pro's Pick Top 12! They also took home the award for Longest Distance (outside of the continental United States).

Driving events were reintroduced at the Nationals last year and proved very popular with muscle car owners. This year entrants and members of the public were given the chance to ride the course for free with a professional driver and lots of people queued up to take advantage of this exciting opportunity.

A highlight of every NSRA Nationals is the drawing of the giveaway street rod and this year it went to a second drawing to find a winner, a local Kentuckian from Shepherdsville, just south of Louisville.

Other popular aspects of the Nationals included the women's reception, the new products display and the swap meet.

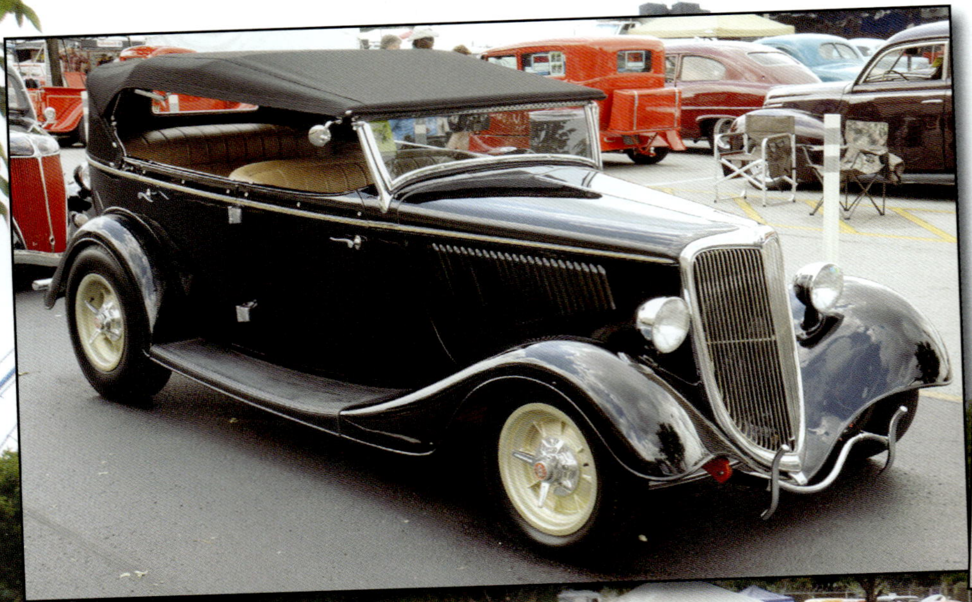

LEFT: Black '34 Ford Phaeton belongs to Jim McPherson from Nashville, Tennessee and was an AMBR contender from earlier in 2017. It features a small block Chevy with vintage sprint car Al Barnes heads and quad-carb injection, Halibrand wheels and a Halibrand quick-change rear end.
BELOW: This low riding and relatively uncommon 1956 Hudson belongs to Lenny Branch from Sullivans Island, South Carolina.

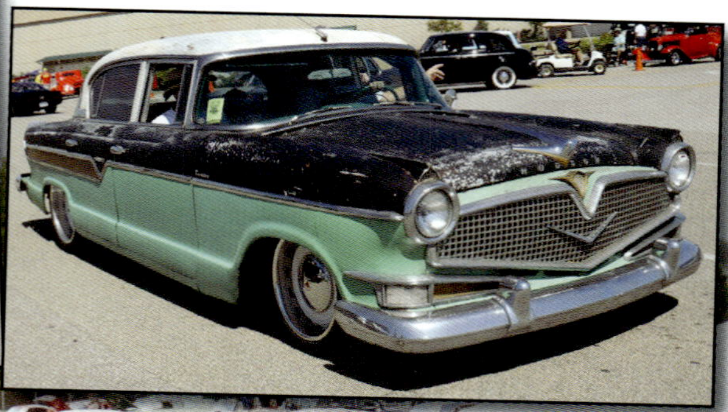

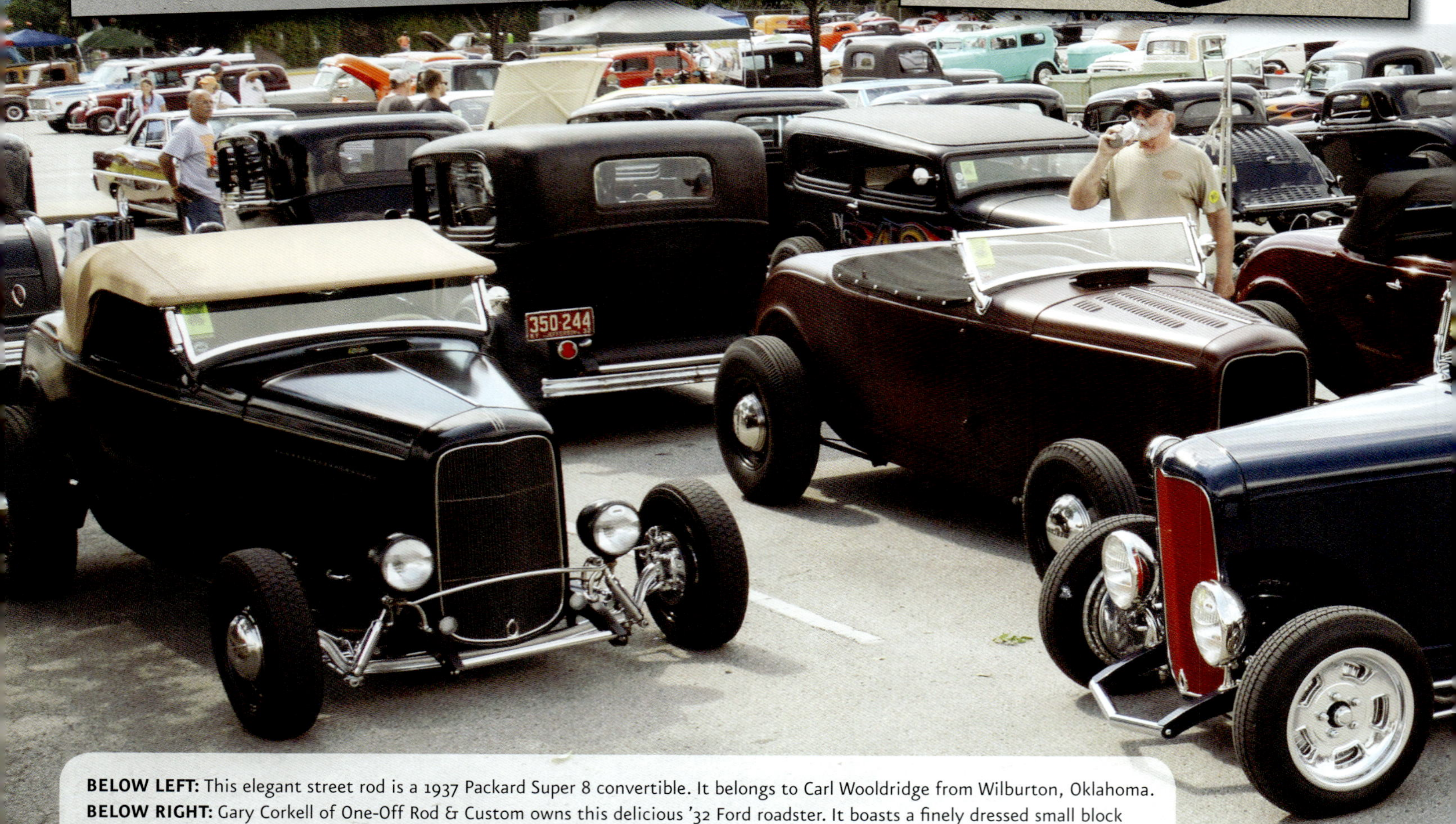

BELOW LEFT: This elegant street rod is a 1937 Packard Super 8 convertible. It belongs to Carl Wooldridge from Wilburton, Oklahoma.
BELOW RIGHT: Gary Corkell of One-Off Rod & Custom owns this delicious '32 Ford roadster. It boasts a finely dressed small block Chevy topped with six carbies and diamond stitched off-white interior trim.

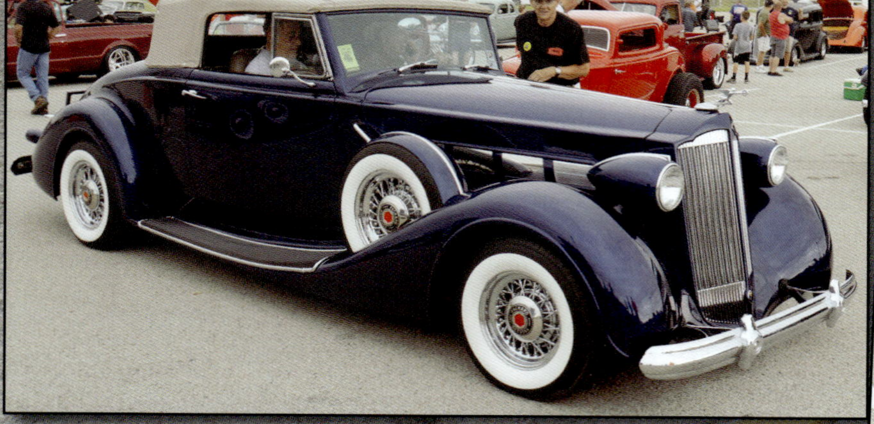

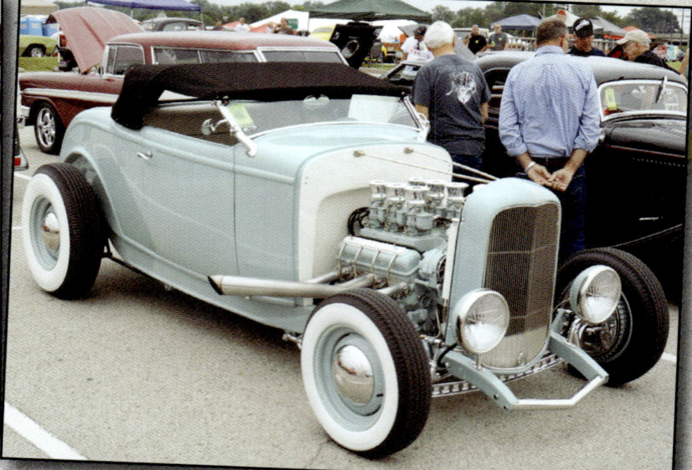

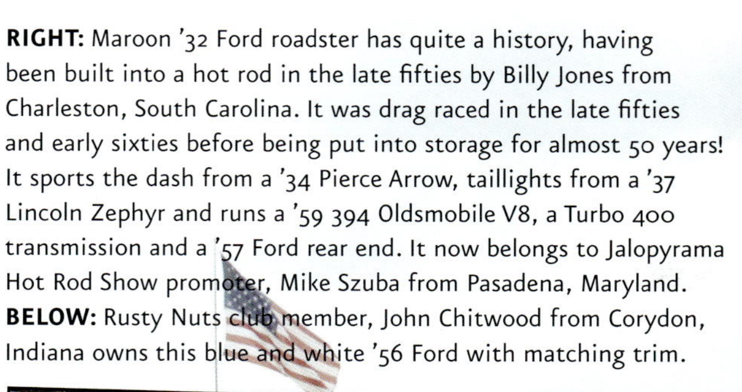

RIGHT: Maroon '32 Ford roadster has quite a history, having been built into a hot rod in the late fifties by Billy Jones from Charleston, South Carolina. It was drag raced in the late fifties and early sixties before being put into storage for almost 50 years! It sports the dash from a '34 Pierce Arrow, taillights from a '37 Lincoln Zephyr and runs a '59 394 Oldsmobile V8, a Turbo 400 transmission and a '57 Ford rear end. It now belongs to Jalopyrama Hot Rod Show promoter, Mike Szuba from Pasadena, Maryland.

BELOW: Rusty Nuts club member, John Chitwood from Corydon, Indiana owns this blue and white '56 Ford with matching trim.

MAIN PIC: Deuce hot rod heaven! From left we have Rick Bales' hiboy roadster from St Peters, Missouri, Andy Pack's '32 from Monticello, Indiana and Don Hansen's maroon Deuce from Rockford, Illinois with Doug Pack's blue version parked in front. The full fendered maroon roadster belongs to Mike Szuba, the black channelled five window coupe was entered by Tommy Grimes from Hodges, Alabama and the chopped Deuce Tudor belongs to Brock Henderson from West Union, Ohio.

BELOW: Mark Nixon from Ironton, Ohio cruising his '28 Model A Ford roadster on Deuce rails. Along with a Moon tank and Deuce grille, it features triple carbies atop a small block mill with open headers and Rocket wheels.

BELOW: Smart, maroon 1940 Ford coupe belongs to Lance Nixon from Grafton, Ohio and sports black and white trim and a tri-powered Chevy.

ABOVE: There were some wild rides in the Builder's Showcase exhibit including this radical 1949 Chevy pickup that was built by Collvins Customs in Mount Vernon, Texas.
LEFT: Brad and Lori Woosley's very tidy '34 Ford Victoria runs a 383 Chevy V8.
BELOW: Americans are a patriotic bunch. Dave and Dee Gilliam from Walton, Kentucky salute their soldiers with this amazingly detailed '46 International delivery.
BOTTOM: Australian hot rodders Roger and Jennifer Vagg took out a Pro's Pick Top 12 trophy along with the award for Longest Distance with their 1932 five window coupe.

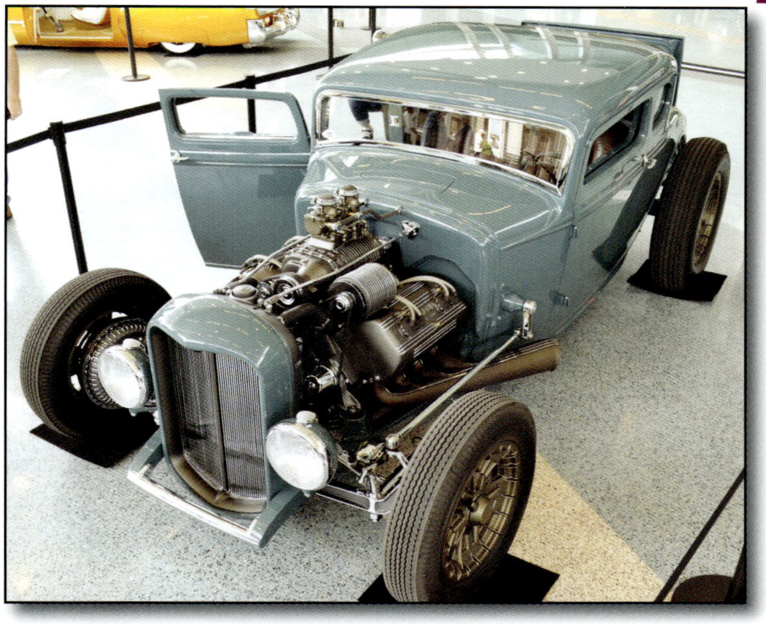

ABOVE: This 1930 Model A coupe, "After Thought" was on display in the Builder's Showcase and was a Ridler contender earlier in the year, gaining Great 8 finalist honours. Mounted on a Deuce chassis and running a blown Ardun equipped flathead, it belongs to Ted and Colleen Hubbard and was built by CAL Automotive Creations.

BELOW: Gary J. Pierre from Glenview, Illinois owns this stunning 1953 DeSoto. It features a 6.1 litre Hemi powerplant, air suspension, Billet Specialties wheels and custom black leather trim with 'gator skin inserts.

ABOVE: This incredible '41 Ford pickup was built by the team at One-Off Rod & Custom and was another 2017 Ridler contender that was on show in the Builder's Showcase exhibition.

BELOW: One of the better finds in the swap meet area was this original and complete '35 Ford three window coupe. Equipped with twin 97s and Offenhauser heads, this flathead powered coupe could have been yours for $35,000.00.

ABOVE: More gold from the swap meet! The orange '41 Ford sedan delivery features a 350/350 combination with a Camaro 10 bolt diff, Mustang II front end and leather trim. It was priced at $42,000.00 while the Deuce coupe was priced at $95,000.00. It was built from an old hot rod by the Rolling Bones Hot Rod Shop in 2006 and uses 383 Chevy power, a TKO600 five speed gearbox and a Halibrand quick-change rear end.

ABOVE: Les and Sandy Sutak from Kingsville, Ontario own this heavily channelled '28 Ford roadster with triple carb equipped big block Chevy running gear.

LEFT: Kyle Cochran travelled up to Louisville from Bowling Green, Kentucky in his wild '48 Dodge pickup. The bare metal truck sits low thanks to air suspension and has plenty of power under the hood thanks to a twin turbo equipped Cummins diesel.

ABOVE: Custom-built '32 Ford woody belongs to local rodders, Mike and Diana Tinsley. Mike built this car in his two car garage using small block Ford running gear.

LEFT: This chopped '32 Ford Victoria caught our attention well before we learned of its long and interesting history. It now belongs to Red and Deb Stauffer of Mount Dora, Florida, but was one of the hottest rods cruising So-Cal streets back in the forties. It belonged to Glendale rodder, Aki Ino and ran a 296ci engine when it clocked 111mph at the first Russetta Timing Association meet in 1946. It was then sold to Bill Coleman of the Glendale Coupe and Roadster Club in 1950. He installed the 239 V8 from his roadster and went 110mph on the dry lakes. It now features magnesium Halibrand wheels, a genuine Ardun equipped flathead V8 running twin carbies and a '36 Ford dash inside with black and white upholstery and a '40 Ford steering wheel. Cool!

BELOW: Hemi powered, channelled '31 Plymouth two door sedan and Brian Arcand's Y Block Ford powered 1930 Model A Ford coupe cruising the fiargrounds.

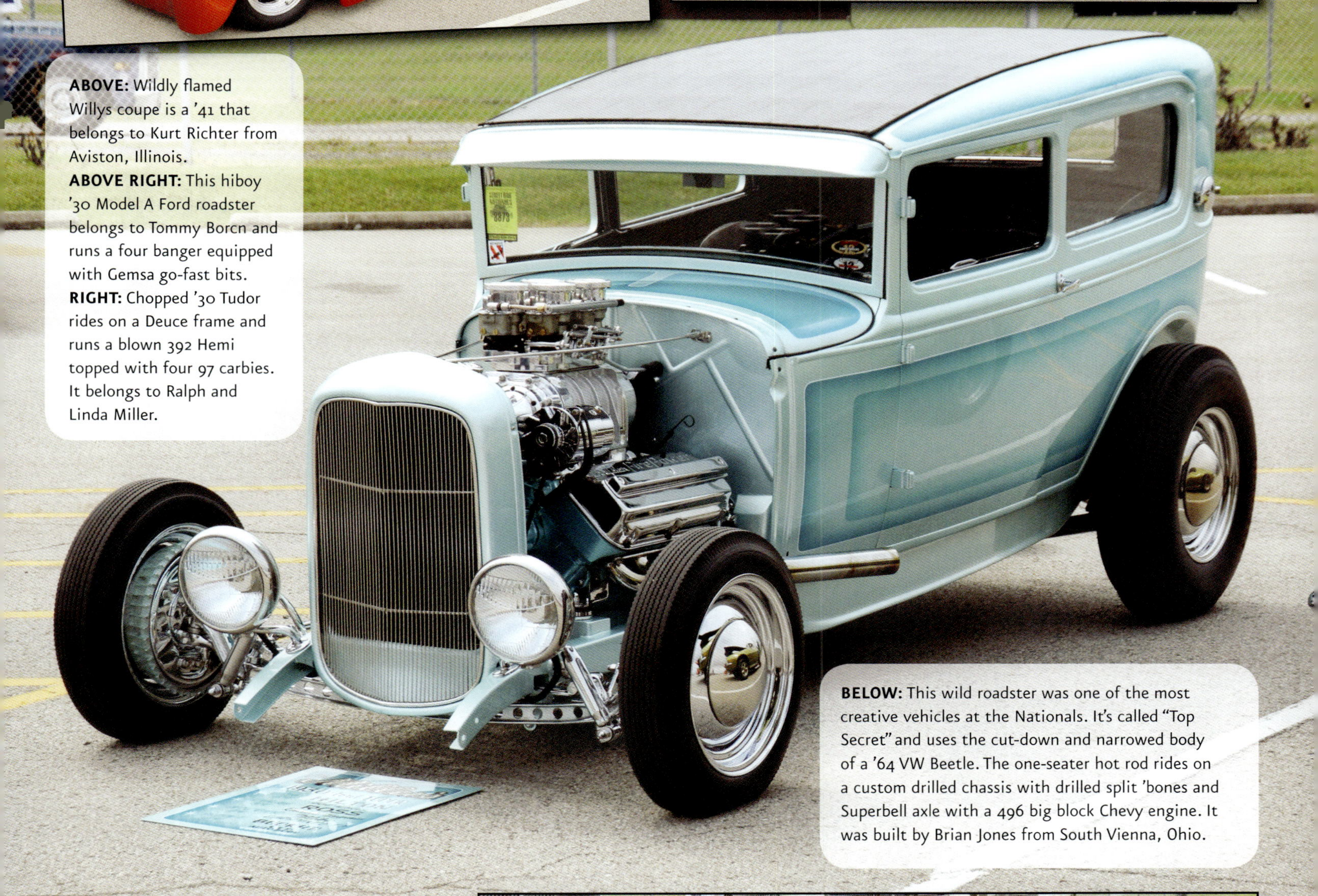

ABOVE: Wildly flamed Willys coupe is a '41 that belongs to Kurt Richter from Aviston, Illinois.

ABOVE RIGHT: This hiboy '30 Model A Ford roadster belongs to Tommy Borcn and runs a four banger equipped with Gemsa go-fast bits.

RIGHT: Chopped '30 Tudor rides on a Deuce frame and runs a blown 392 Hemi topped with four 97 carbies. It belongs to Ralph and Linda Miller.

BELOW: This wild roadster was one of the most creative vehicles at the Nationals. It's called "Top Secret" and uses the cut-down and narrowed body of a '64 VW Beetle. The one-seater hot rod rides on a custom drilled chassis with drilled split 'bones and Superbell axle with a 496 big block Chevy engine. It was built by Brian Jones from South Vienna, Ohio.

ABOVE: George Poteet owns many remarkable cars and this '32 Ford Tudor, built by Johnson's Hot Rod Shop, is no exception. This car made the Great 8 at the Detroit Autorama and runs Y block power, side-steering and a quick-change diff.
BELOW: This 409 big block powered '69 Camaro with a Corvair roof belongs to Michael and Felice Feinstein. It also uses a '61 Chev Belair dash and wheel.

ABOVE: Sharp '48 Bentley saloon is a refreshing car as a street rod and really looks the part with dark tinted glass, whitewalls on wide chrome wheels and rich cream paint. Owners are Lyle and Kathy Smith from Trantville, Virginia.
BELOW: Matt blue and flamed '32 Ford Tudor also has a top chop and small block Chevy engine. It was driven in by Dale Grau from Rice, Minnesota.

ABOVE: What better way to enjoy the glorious weather that was a feature of the Nationals than to cruise the fairgrounds in Chad Adams' slick six cylinder powered Deuce tourer.

TOP: Driving events made a comeback at the NSRA Nationals in 2016 and they were popular again in 2017. Here Chris King puts his 408 cube LS small-block powered '69 Camaro through its paces in the streetkhana.

ABOVE & ABOVE RIGHT: Darrell Cimbanin's black '29 Model A roadster oozes appeal with its trimmed bomber style interior super low overall stance and full Moon discs on the wheels. There's an LS Chevy in the engine bay, a dropped headlight bar up front and frameless windshield aiding the clean appearance.

RIGHT: Blacked out satin finish '54 Chevy delivery is a trend-setting style that is catching on fast. The air-bag equipped beauty is owned by Brent Wagner.

BELOW RIGHT: That's a hot rodded 1948 British Riley fitted with Chevy running gear. It belongs to Sue Sanders from Paducah, Kentucky.

BELOW: Period style '31 Model A Ford coupe has Y block Ford running gear, mild top chop and blackwall tyres on unusual steel wheels. This one is owned by Nathan and Jim Stewart from the Buckeye Rod Builders in Sunbury, Ohio.

Rattle Trap
Crowdy Head, NSW

WORDS & PHOTOS: SHOW N GO PHOTOGRAPHY

TOP LEFT: James Minas faces the starter in his T special, John Viles blasts off in his vinyl covered '26 Dodge roadster and Clinton Horne tries out his green Model A Ford special.

www.graffitipub.com.au

Different criteria come into play when you want to race on a beach! The Drag-ens Hot Rod Club from Sydney organised the first such event for many long years when they descended on Crowdy Head near Taree, NSW for their inaugural Rattletrap beach racing event. Such racing is entirely dependent on taking advantage of the time lapse between outgoing and incoming tides so the whole event had to be structured around that window of opportunity. Calculations indicated that there would be about a four hour period available on the chosen date.

Before the event could get under way there were provisions to be put in place and that all started with meetings to get permits in place and to get the local caravan parks, Lions club and surf club involved. Once this was all settled the start of racing on the day was scheduled from 9:00am to 2:00pm. A limited number of entrants was agreed upon to allow them all to get in enough passes on the day to make the event a success. Entrant vehicles had to be non-blower, fuel injected nor turbo-charged motors and could only be early 1920s up to 1941 makes and models, including bikes to the 1960s. On the day they were able to run about 20 cars and approximately eight motor bikes.

There was a huge crowd of spectators and 200-300 street rods in the car park, so the first Rattletrap was deemed a great success. Top Hot Rod went to Deano Webb, Top Bike was awarded to Zac Ralph, the Surf Club picked a red Ford Model A Tudor for the Car Park Choice and Best Dressed winners were David Lance and partner.

Rattletrap #2 is scheduled Crowdy Head Beach again on May 12, 2018.

ABOVE: Timeless picture of the staging lanes could have been taken 50 years ago. In the foreground is Rod Brewer's radically chopped '34 Ford three window coupe with quick-change diff visible under the rear and hairpin front radius rods. Runs had to be made between the turn of the tides so organisation had to be spot on with minimum tIme wasted between each dash across the beach.

TOP: The racing day started with a competitors meeting to outline procedures so that everyone could enjoy the day.
ABOVE: Paul McMullin had two cars at the Rattletrap, his '32 Ford hiboy roadster getting away smartly here against his red Ford V8 special.

ABOVE: Mason Cahill roars away from the start in his 265 Hemi six cylinder powered T bucket.

ABOVE: Drag-Ens officials hand out timing slips to a couple of the racers.
BELOW: Another timeless picture, thanks to mono reproduction and Corey Longfield's period styled '41 Ford coupe.

ABOVE: To keep things running smoothly a batch of cars were took a turn to run through the measured track, and then all returned at once, so that a maximum number of runs could be made in the restricted racing window between tide movements.
BOTTOM LEFT: Wise Guys club member Frankie Pana sprays up the sand as he launches his 21 stud flathead powered Deuce roadster from the start line.
BOTTOM RIGHT: Quick-change equipped '32 Ford hiboy roadster also has flathead power and is owned by Matt Teece.

MAIN PIC: Leaping flag starter Alicia O'Bryan sends another two beach racers on their way.
BOTTOM LEFT: Number 28 is Doug Sterry's '28 Model A Ford based racer charging away from the start line while racing Ashley Swift in the Model A tourer.
BOTTOM RIGHT: Severely chopped and channelled '30 Model A Ford sedan of Lee Holt has tractor grille and power enough to churn the Crowdy Head beach sand. The timing tower in the background was built especially for the event.

LEFT: Beautiful black and white shot of James Minas' T special and Phil Bond's channelled Model A Ford roadster competing against each other.
BELOW: Looking back at the staging lanes reveals a field of nostalgia styled hot rods awaiting their turn to blast the beach.
BELOW LEFT: Doug Sterry's Model A Ford roadster puts a hole-shot on Paul Garrat's '30 Model A Ford coupe.

BELOW: On the return "road" we have the roadster pickup of Ryan Lofts, the #28 speedster of Doug Sterry and Frankie Pana's satin black Deuce roadster.

www.graffitipub.com.au

Top Hot Rod: Deano Webb.
Top Bike: Zac Ralph.
Surf Club Car Park Choice: Red Ford Tudor.
Surf Club Best Dressed: David Lance and Partner.

ABOVE: Craig Fischer's Model A roadster is nicer than many but he wasn't afraid to hurl it down the beach strip.

BELOW: The criteria for entry allowed for bobber style bikes to enjoy some of the fun in the sand.
RIGHT: Another bike racer takes his turn at facing the starter for a blast down the beach strip.

Real Hot Rod!

John Martin
Nixa, Missouri, USA
1934 Ford Five Window Coupe

Story: Larry O'Toole
Photos: Al O'Toole & John Martin

John Martin grew up in the perfect era. He started high school in 1954 when rock and roll was just beginning. In the late '50s and early '60s, hot rodders were taking their cars off the street, installing all the horsepower they could find, and heading for the drag strip. This remains John's idea of a real hot rod.

John's '34 Ford five window coupe is designed to reflect those times, but with the latest horsepower and safety equipment. The body is beautifully finished with a four inch tapered chop, laid-back windshield, laid-forward rear of the roof and custom made firewall. The fuel tank and radiator take up all of the trunk space where there is no trunk floor.

The chassis and running gear features the finest safety equipment, all SFI approved, and the chrome moly roll cage was built by Jim Wiens Race Cars and is NHRA certified. Inside, the Speedway bomber seats are upholstered in leather.

It's the engine in this beast that grabs your attention. John used an all-aluminum New Century Performance block topped by Brodix "Big Duke" heads. An Ohio Crankshaft stroker crank and rods hold Diamond pistons and the 4.56 inch bore combined with the 5.3 inch stroker crank results in a monstrous 693 cubic inches.

A Kinsler/Mercury Marine stack injection system was converted to electronic control with a FAST 2.0 computer supplying 16 injectors. New Century Performance custom-machined the plenum in the stacks to make tuning more forgiving. The valve train is all from Comp Cams with the exception of T&D shaft-mounted rocker arms and Trend tapered push rods.

The engine is cammed conservatively to make sure the beast is streetable. Nevertheless it still produces 818 ft. lbs. of torque at 4250 rpm and 825 hp at 6000 rpm. The SW Powerglide transmission seems hardly necessary due to the incredible torque. A Strange nine inch Ford rear end finishes out the driveline.

John is a physicist who has always worked as a mechanical engineer because he is such a motor head. The '34 shows evidence of some safety conscious engineering you don't usually see on American street rods. For example, John designed a collapsible steering column and front and rear-mounted cameras. He also plans to utilise traction control as soon as he figures out how to do it. All controls are in easy reach of the driver when he is strapped into the five-point Stroud harness.

The coupe is on the heavy side, due to the leather interior and heavier than usual chassis, but John and New Century Performance estimate it will run high eights or low nines at the drag strip when fitted with a set of Mickey Thompson slicks. John designed a plug-in Stroud parachute system to make sure he can stop the car. It should be a fun ride!

JOHN'S ROD SHOP
1934

Real Hot Rod!

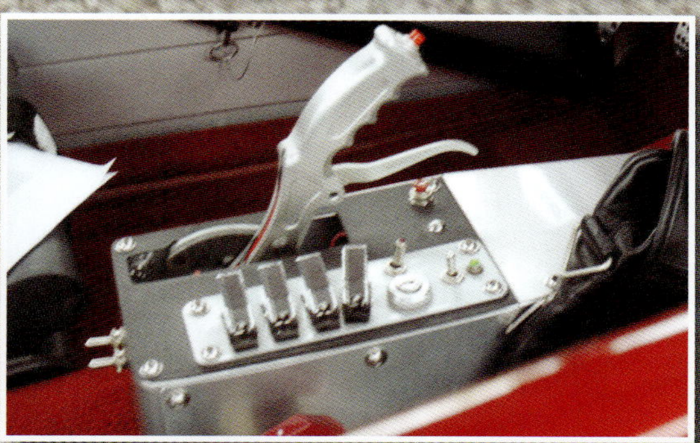

Speed Week 2017
THE BONNEVILLE ALBUM

Words and Photos: Al O'Toole

LAKE BONNEVILLE, UTAH, USA

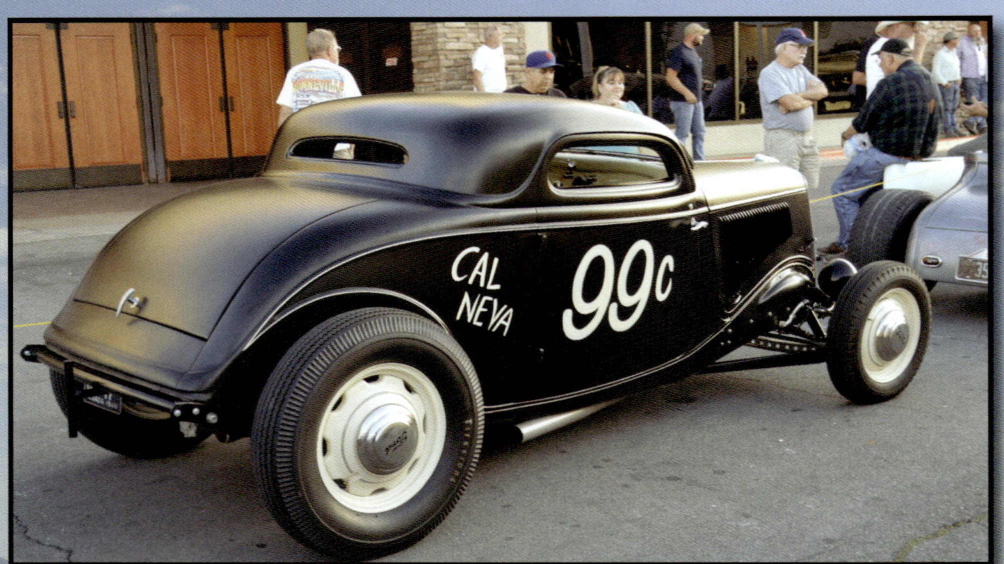

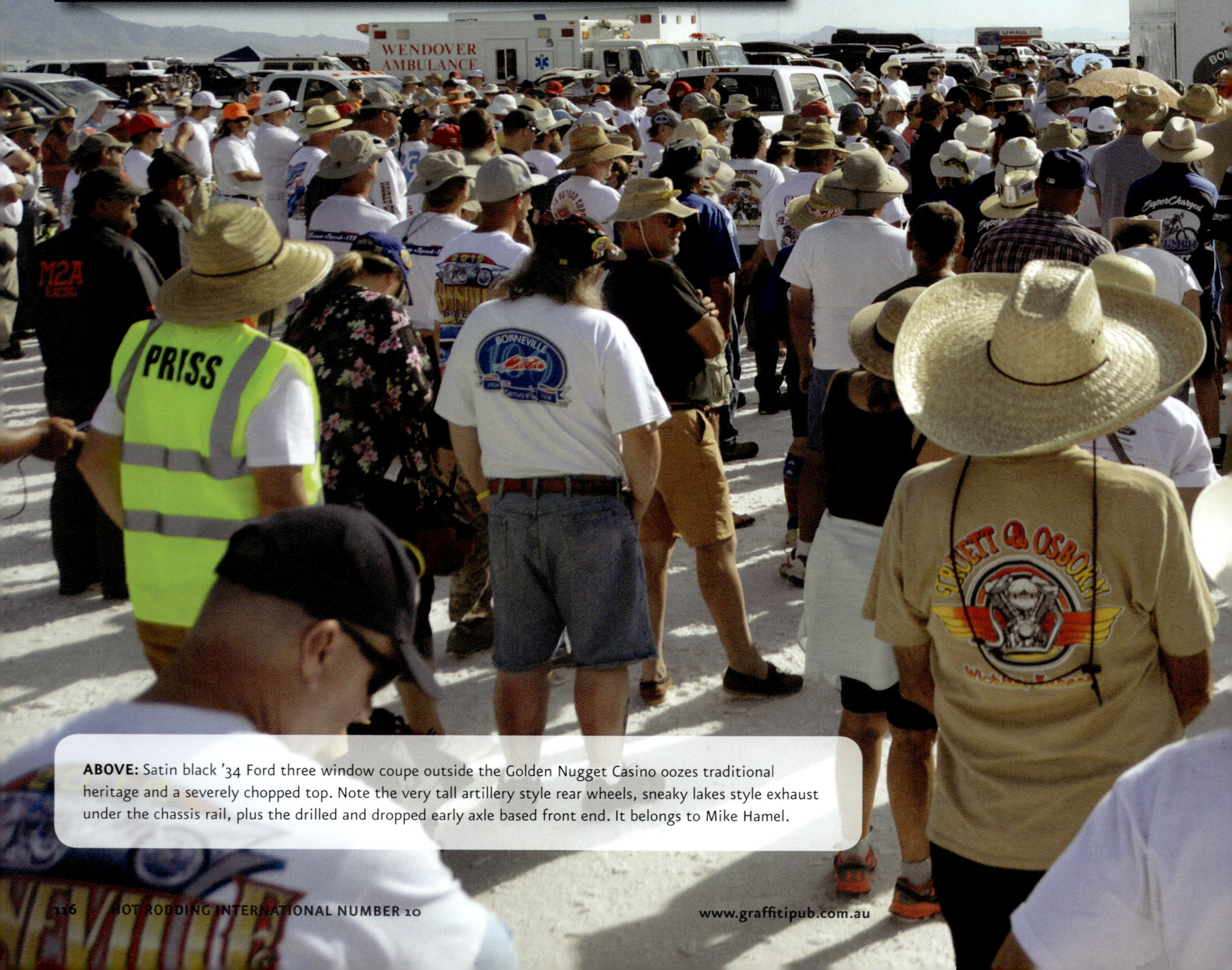

ABOVE: Satin black '34 Ford three window coupe outside the Golden Nugget Casino oozes traditional heritage and a severely chopped top. Note the very tall artillery style rear wheels, sneaky lakes style exhaust under the chassis rail, plus the drilled and dropped early axle based front end. It belongs to Mike Hamel.

Despite a rough racing surface, the 69th Bonneville Speed Week was still a great success with dozens of new records set and many personal best runs completed by the 548 entries that turned up to the great white dyno.

Three courses were graded for Speed Week 2017, one long course, one short course and a rookie track for the first timers. On Saturday morning racing got underway with the honorary first pass by Mike "Nick" Nicholas in his historic, dual engine Model A pickup "Odd Rod", followed soon after by both George Poteet and Danny Thompson charging down the salt one after the other at over 400 mph! It's always cool to watch guys like this prepare for such a run at the start line, but to watch a dry lakes racer speed past the pits at full noise is an experience one has to witness in person to truly appreciate it. It's exciting, loud and so incredible to watch that it just doesn't seem natural for something to move across the earth at such jaw-dropping speeds. Poteet ended up winning the Fastest Time of the Meet trophy with a 438.643 mph run. Thompson was a close second, running his "Challenger II" streamliner to a top speed of 435.735 mph!

By the end of the week, 93 new records had been set, 11 drivers were inducted into the "200 mph Club" and one made it into the prestigious "300 Chapter". Mike Strasburg scored an elusive blue hat by steering the Wolfe/Strasburg/Hiltunen AA blown fuel lakester to a new record of 344.126 mph!

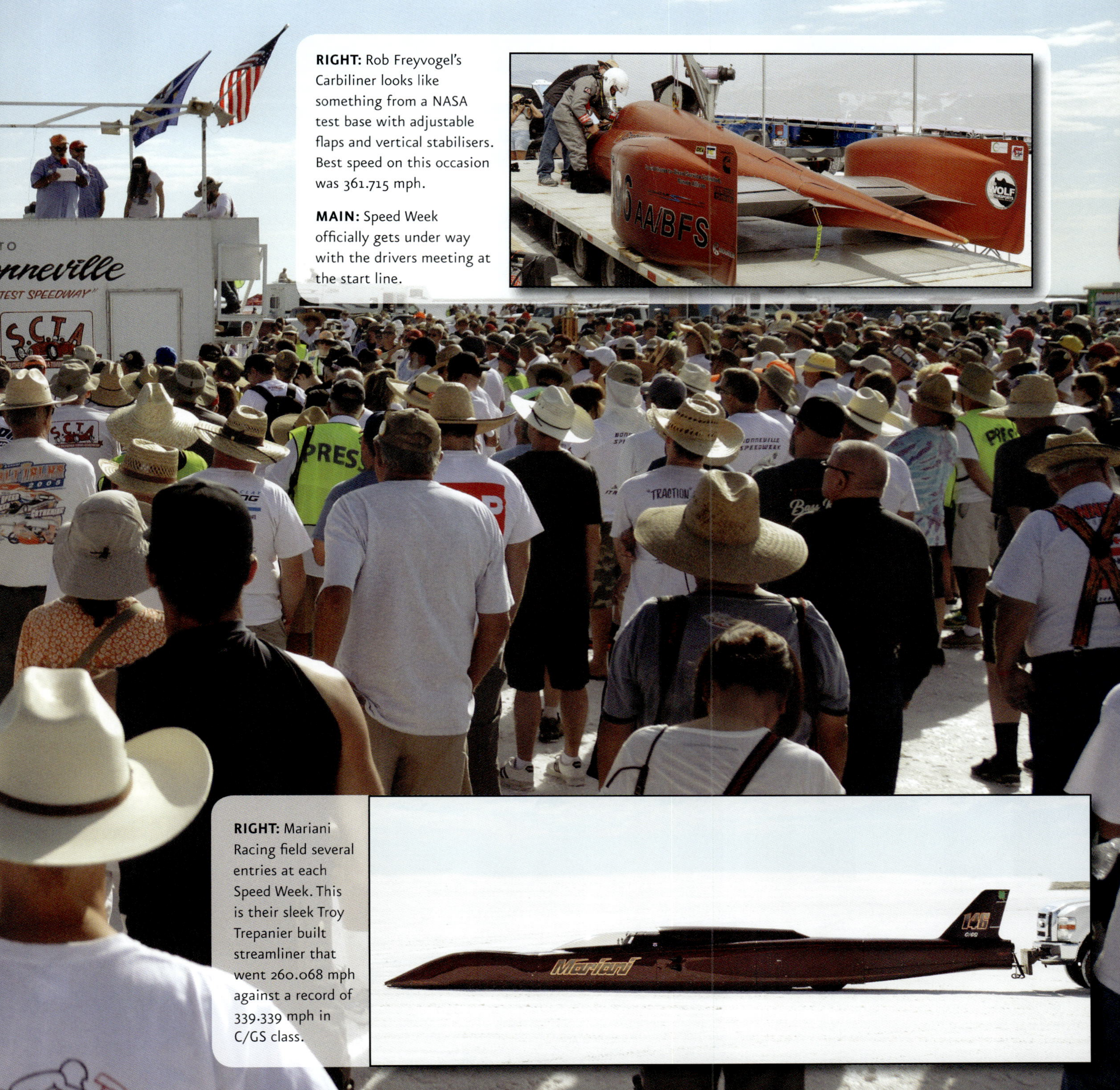

RIGHT: Rob Freyvogel's Carbiliner looks like something from a NASA test base with adjustable flaps and vertical stabilisers. Best speed on this occasion was 361.715 mph.

MAIN: Speed Week officially gets under way with the drivers meeting at the start line.

RIGHT: Mariani Racing field several entries at each Speed Week. This is their sleek Troy Trepanier built streamliner that went 260.068 mph against a record of 339.339 mph in C/GS class.

ABOVE: Panel painted T roadster appears to have been made from a coupe. It sits front and centre outside the Golden Nugget Casino for all to admire.

MAIN: Always a big attraction at the after racing show outside the Golden Nugget Casino is the display of rods from the Rolling Bones Garage. They have the early lakes style of hot rod build perfected.

ABOVE: Time to front the starter for another run down the salt. Crew members push Greg Waters in the White Goose Bar Racing Team's Model A roadster that uses a Toyota six cylinder engine.

ABOVE: The Vescoe & ATS Team pushes the Turbinator II streamliner up to the start line for an attempt at the 427.832 mph record. They managed 385.448 mph this year.
RIGHT: Driver Eric Ritter is prepared for the run before stepping into the cockpit of the Turbinator II, one of the fastest streamliners on the salt.
BELOW RIGHT: Everyone has fun at Bonneville, not the least those who drive their hot rods into the desert for a week of racing and camaraderie.

ABOVE: Bare metal chopped and dropped two door Chevy rests on the pavement outside the Golden Nugget Casino.

ABOVE LEFT: Everyone brings something different to the salt. This low profile bike in the back of a pickup truck attracted its fair share of attention.

ABOVE: Channelled '32 Ford roadster with flathead engine and early wire wheels conjures up images of a true "beater" style hot rod.
MAIN: Under starter's instructions is the F/BGR Model A roadster of the White Goose Bar Racing Team of Waters/Manghelli/Romero. Consistency was a problem but they managed to post a 202.881 mph pass with early shut-off.

ABOVE: Unusual '37 Ford pickup based wagon means the whole crew can travel together – and with nothing less than Hemi power up front.

BELOW: Classic profile of a chopped Deuce hiboy Tudor reveals quick-change rear end and period style pinstriping. It runs small block Chevy running gear and fits right in at Speed Week. This one belongs to Dale Grau from Rice, Minnesota.

BELOW: Even the right style show car is welcome at Speed Week. Allan Winward's semi-custom '36 Ford five window coupe is typical with its flathead engine and '40 Ford dash.

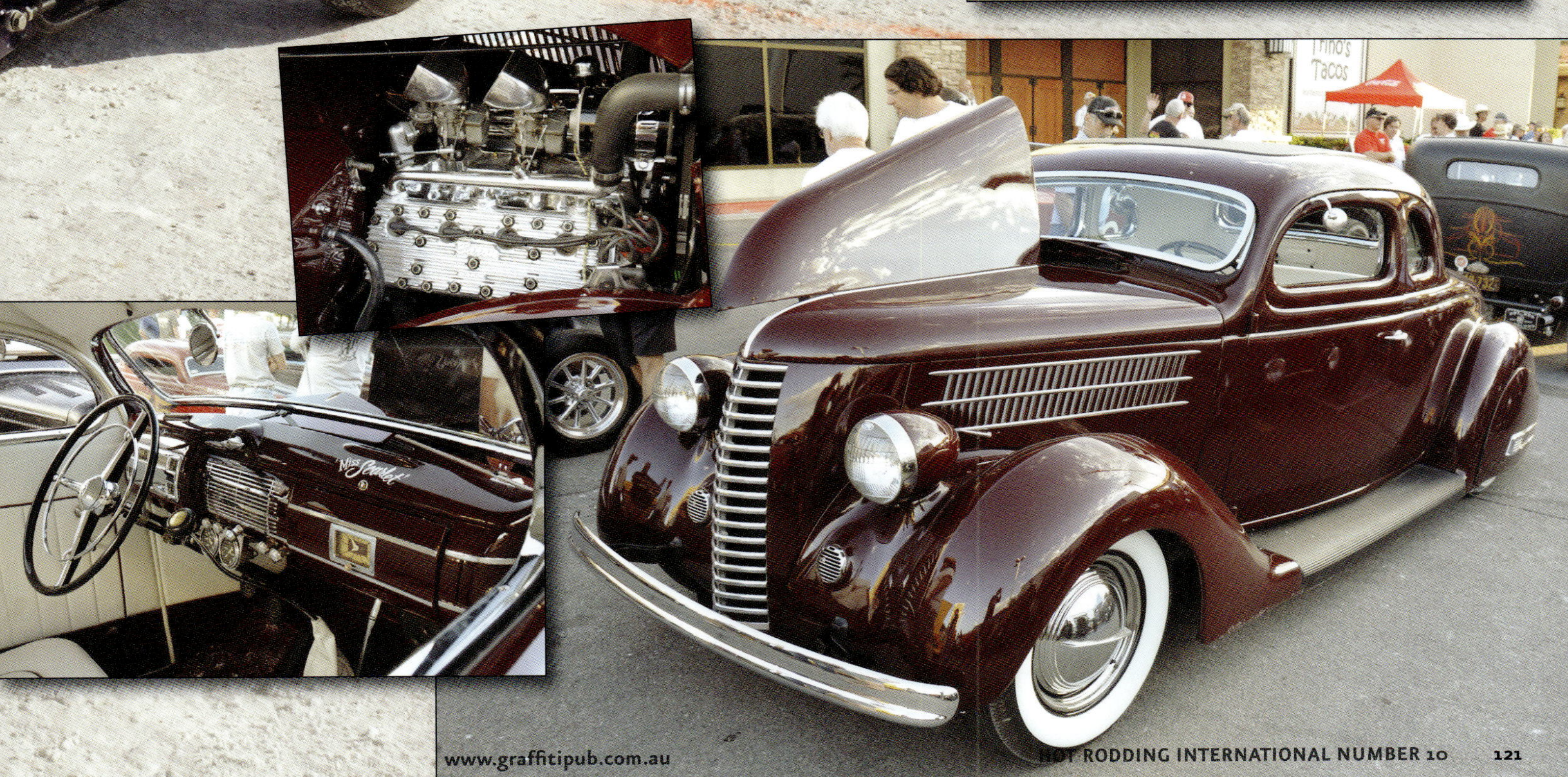

ABOVE & LEFT: Cook Racing Team came all the way from New Zealand for a crack at the G/FS racing record and pushed it up to 260.363 mph.

ABOVE: You can't get the side profile of a '36 Ford cabriolet much lower than this example. It has the body sectioned and channelled over the frame, but remains full fendered.

BELOW: Street driven modifieds look fantastic on the pure white salt. This little buzz-box uses nicely detailed flathead Ford V8 running gear.

MAIN: What fun there is to be had with an old T Ford based modified like this "boat-back" special.

LEFT: A DeSoto Airflow can only be described as rare, especially when it is a coupe. This one raced by the 404 Team uses a blown straight eight engine.

www.graffitipub.com.au

RIGHT: Danny Thompson rests contemplatively against the transporter while crew ready the Challenger II streamliner for a record qualifying run of 435.735 mph.

BELOW: Blowfish has been racing for several years but still looks immaculate. It was built for salt lake legend George Poteet by Troy Trepanier and on this occasion went 200.632 mph with Jason McOlgan in the driver's seat.

ABOVE: Neat Model A roadster pickup has earned its salt spray initiation with small block Ford running gear. The front plate tells you the owner is part of the "Roads End Gang", a reference to the camping area on the way out to the salt races.

ABOVE: There's nothing quite as impressive as a sleek streamliner and the "Saltwinder" is a perfect example.

LEFT: Classic McCulloch supercharger fed by a pair of Stromberg 97s hang off a four banger engine in a '31 Model A Ford.

BELOW: Unusual truck based rod with a custom made nose section was for sale in the casino parking lot.

BOTTOM: The Renck, Hull, Bottini and Roberts Model A roadster is low, sleek and handsome. Running in C/GR class it went 226.463 mph.

RIGHT: Take a GMC six, add puff and stuff it in a Bantam roadster and you have a typical salt lake racer. This one is owned by the Goldman Racing Team and went 219.111 mph for a new record in XXO BFMR class. That's haulin' for a vintage engine.

LEFT: Taking its place outside the Golden Nugget Casino is this low slung Model T Ford roadster with appropriate display of pictures for sale standing along the chassis rail.

RIGHT: Don Dillard has been driving his chopped '30 Model A coupe to Bonneville for years.

FAR RIGHT: Radically low and chopped Model A coupe has a fat Hemi stuffed in the engine bay with a trio of Holley 94 carbies on a custom made intake manifold perched on top.

MAIN: Time for one more streamliner, this time the black and white arrow of the Hardman Racing Team that used Dodge power to go 274.708 mph in F/BGS class.

SPEED WEEK RESULTS

Vehicle	Entry Name	Engine Body	New Record	Driver Name
7	Aardema - Braun	F FRMR	211.218	Cal Rothe
60	Fast Four Special	V4F BFMR	150.141	Peter Henderickson
84	So What Speed Shop	A BGRMR	157.503	Shug Hanchard
181	Chris Mursick	G CFALT	113.358	Chris Mursick
218	EightInARow Racing	XO BGR	147.965	Randall Foehner
285	BMR Ferguson Racing	XXF BFCC	197.446	Neil McAlister
302	Goldman Racing	XXO BFMR	219.111	Garret Boyle
351	Little Bastards	XXF BFRMR	164.126	Jim Lindsay
506	Wolfe-Strasburg	AA BFL	344.126	Mike Strasburg
622	Salty Box Racing	B DT	204.498	Tim Boyle
622	Salty Box Racing	B DT	208.232	Jason Simson
622	Salty Box Racing	B DT	206.466	Ryan Boyle
622	Salty Box Racing	B DT	198.013	Tim Boyle
651	Richard Smith	AA BFCC	250.827	Richard Smith
688	Lil Bit O Racing	D MP	162.498	Larry Lancaster
715	Speed Demon Racing	A BFS	423.521	George Poteet
743	McFaddin & Loyd	E CBGALT	207.313	John Loyd
883	Rick Harden	A BFMS	261.945	Rick Harden
1285	BMR Ferguson Racing	XXF BVFCC	200.718	Neil McAlister
1326	MKM Racingo	H BFRMR	190.352	Mike Borders
1337	Greenspeed Research	C DT	219.411	Dave Schenker
1707	Victory Motorsports	F DS	212.746	Burton Brown
1811	Chris Mursick	G CGALT	124.611	Chris Mursick
1839	Class of 39	XXF FALT	114.754	Ryan Krejc
1916	Thomas & Dean Thunde	AA FRMR	234.663	Brian Dean
1937	Mitchell Motorsports	XXO VGALT	160.875	Roger Mitchell
1939	Class of 39	XXF BGALT	135.066	Mark Lichtenwalter
3663	Blake Machine 36 Buick	XO GCC	175.031	Brian Blake
4449	Jesel Landspeed Team	AA MP	219.749	Jimmy Shine
5810	Mark Ortiz	G CBFALT	146.715	Mark Ortiz
5811	Mark Ortiz	G CBGALT	134.606	Mark Ortiz
5844	Rick Deerwester	G CPRO	145.632	Rick Deerwester
5844	Rick Deerwester	G CPRO	144.697	Rick Deerwester
6832	Reg Cook	G FS	260.363	Steve Davies
7010	Bukshy Racing	E CBGC	156.369	Steve Rutherford
8150	Ron's Hobby Shop Special	XXF BGRMR	216.131	Ron San Giovanni Sr
8150	Ron's Hobby Shop Special	XXF BGRMR	225.003	Ron San Giovanni Sr
9260	John Ballantyne	V4F BFR	144.091	John Ballantyne
9278	Landjet	E CPS	140.633	Dan Haugh
9991	Salt Cat Racing	XO BFALT	180.403	Dave Grieve
9997	Salt Cat Racing	XO BGC	159.110	Doug Grieve
4B	Team McLeish Bros	1350CC SCS-F	170.797	Derek McLeish
113B	Alp Racing & Design	650CC APS-VF	135.724	Alp Sungurtekin
286B	Puckett LSR	125CC MPS-BG	52.656	John Thurston
372B	Team Bucket 372B	100CC A-BG	91.045	Tim Lewis
372B	Team Bucket 372B	100CC A-BG	87.472	Tim Lewis
372B	Team Bucket 372B	100CC A-BG	71.277	Tim Lewis
372B	Team Bucket 372B	100CC A-BG	84.622	Tim Lewis

SPEED WEEK RESULTS

Vehicle	Entry Name	Engine Body	New Record	Driver Name
460B	Puckett LSR	250CC MPS-PBG	76.814	Frank Puckett
461B	Puckett LSR	250CC MPS-PBF	74.380	Dana Robbins
488B	Team Threshing Machine	500CC APS-VBF	105.335	Martin Willmott
488B	Team Threshing Machine	500CC APS-VBF	118.974	Martin Willmott
626B	Hal Tacker / Overkill	175CC MPS-BF	88.408	Hal Tacker
646B	Falkirk Salt Flats Team	650CC MPS-PBG	101.259	Neil McDonald
685B	H. Alex Balogi	750CC P-PP	127.301	Alex Balogi
734B	Chkalov Team	350CC MPS-VG	88.995	Maksym Saydiiev
775B	Dave Branch & Steve French	750CC APS-PBF	152.358	Steve French
775B	Dave Branch & Steve French	750CC APS-PBF	151.540	Steve French
784B	Kmamk Team	650CC M-PBG	73.041	Serhii Malyk
797B	Jean-Paul Afflick	100CC APS-BF	95.716	Jean-Paul Afflick
797B	Jean-Paul Afflick	100CC APS-BF	101.332	Jean-Paul Afflick
797B	Jean-Paul Afflick	100CC APS-BF	111.344	Jean-Paul Afflick
797B	Jean-Paul Afflick	100CC APS-BF	107.808	Jean-Paul Afflick
930B	Speranza Brandt Robinson	1350CC SC-PBG	177.316	Randy Speranza
944B	Speranza Brandt Robinson	1350CC SCS-PBF	174.820	Randy Speranza
1115B	Puckett LSR	100CC SC-BG	43.883	Frank Puckett
1137B	Stinky Bean MWG	1000CC SC-VG	64.522	William Paulovcin
1433B	Diamond Mob	650CC A-PBG	124.059	Chris Hawkshaw
1433B	Diamond Mob	650CC A-PBG	125.617	Chris Hawkshaw
1433B	Diamond Mob	650CC A-PBG	110.820	Chris Hawkshaw
1433B	Diamond Mob	650CC A-PBG	127.338	Chris Hawkshaw
1586B	Puckett LSR	100CC M-BF	47.814	Jim Lefever
1800B	Gold Wing Lyon	2000CC SC-BG	111.716	Christine Creel
2202B	Team Danny Macias	350CC M-PF	94.922	George Nachtsheim
2205B	Inspirium ICM	350CC APS-VG	99.764	Dmytro Bagryantsev
2441B	Speranza Brandt Robinson	1350CC APS-PBG	168.342	Raudy Speranza
2813B	Rabbit Foot Racing	1350CC P-PV	102.404	Zachery Waters
3286B	Puckett LSR	125CC MPS-BF	45.012	Maria Gevber
3411B	Guthrie / Levie Racing	750CC SC-BG	170.415	Allen Levie
3413B	Guthrie-Levie Racing	175CC MPS-BF	100.781	John Levie
3413B	Guthrie-Levie Racing	175CC MPS-BF	84.415	John Levie
3414B	Guthrie / Levie Racing	750CC SC-BF	172.034	Allen Levie
3414B	Guthrie / Levie Racing	750CC SC-BF	138.195	Allen Levie
3415B	Guthrie / Levie Racing	175CC M-BG	82.739	John Levie
3416B	Guthrie Levie Racing	175CC M-BF	77.692	John Levie
3416B	Guthrie Levie Racing	175CC M-BF	90.506	John Levie
6262B	Overkill - Hal Tracker	175CC M-BF	84.495	Hal Tacker
6668B	Black AJS Racing 2	500CC SC-F	85.407	John Dorn
7134B	Performance Indian	1000CC A-VG	136.897	Craig Murray
7771B	Mason Mattocks	175CC P-PV	62.663	Mason Mattocks
7847B	AMR	500CC M-PBF	135.701	Sean Miller
9441B	Speranza Brandt Robinson	1350CC APS-PBF	168.588	Randy Speranza
9691B	Bottle Fed Racing	50CC APS-F	91.517	Todd Moen

KUMEU
CLASSIC CAR
AND
HOT ROD
FESTIVAL
New Zealand
Kumeu Classic Car and Hot Rod Festival
Words & Photos: Greg Stokes
Ford
V8

ABOVE: First rodded in the fifties, Mike Udjur's 1932 Ford roadster is just as it appeared on the cover of the July 1976 New Zealand Hot Rod Magazine.

ABOVE: Aaron Carson's T roadster draws inspiration from the Tommy Ivo bucket of the fifties. Note the rare mechanical Hilborn injected Ford engine.

MAIN: John Goodall specialises in Ford F100 pickups and had these reasonably priced examples available. The blue one was $45,000.00 and the black one $25,000.00.

Just shy of 25 years, the annual Kumeu Hot Rod & Classic Car Festival in West Auckland, New Zealand has been a "must do" on the automotive calendar. Founded by the New Zealand NSRA and now privately promoted by long time rodders, Ken and Desma Galvin, the car show and swap meet weekend attracts enthusiasts from all over New Zealand.

The Kumeu Hot Rod & Classic Car Festival has evolved so much over the years with an interest to cater to such a wide variety of people. It's now become an event which will have some enjoyable aspects to it for the die-hard car enthusiast and some aspects to those who enjoy food and music festivals. Either way you want to look at it, it's best to take of it what you want and enjoy the event for how it interests you.

TOP: The West Auckland Engine Reconditioners T bucket carries a healthy Chrysler Hemi engine and the "FSTFSH" early Barracuda is a perfect example of the breed.

ABOVE: Rods by Reid displayed their world class products and services to their usual high standard. This year the feature was a Deuce chassis, ready to roll with quick-change rear end and finned brakes.

ABOVE RIGHT: One for the Shelby lovers, a GT 390 in perfectly restored and improved condition.

RIGHT How about a 1919 Model T tourer with repaired body, new wood and heaps more spares at home? It could have been your new project for $12,000.00.

LEFT: Tony House' and Dan Tyler's Model A roadsters hanging out at the Rocket Speed Equipment stand.

BELOW LEFT: Murray Frank's Model T coupe is a real blast from the past with Y block Ford engine and unusual twin carby arrangement. The pickup was sourced in Mexico by Squeak Bell.

BELOW: Warwick Dawes' rare 1946 Chev convertible is one of the most tasteful resto rods we have seen lately. It features all Jaguar independent suspension and Warwick runs with East Bay Rods.

LEFT: From East Bay Rods, Richard Grogan's Ford Bonus is tastefully done with a range of custom styling touches.

ABOVE: Plenty of potential power in this twin tunnel ram equipped, big block Chevy motivated '53 Studebaker. Owner Murray Halstead is the King of the Studebakers in New Zealand.

LEFT: Twin turbochargers on a small block Chevy engine should wake up the performance potential in Jack Rainbow's slammed Chevy C10 pickup. The truck has distinctive green painted roof, making it stand out in a crowd.

ABOVE LEFT: Magoo's Street Rods have added a 1932 Ford five window coupe to their reproduction fibreglass body range. This aqua display car with injected small block Chevy V8 and a new set of American Racing five spokes would be a good option for someone wanting to start a project.

ABOVE: Peter Jenkins' cool cruiser is this neat '37 Ford Tudor ex USA rolling on Merc rims with trim rings and whitewall tyres.

LEFT: Simon Clements' tough '32 Ford Tudor is at home on the drag strip as it is on the street with a big block Chev for power. The primer grey Tudor has a roll bar and Halibrand front wheels that all add to the old style race theme.

BELOW Veteran & Vintage Cars had this cool Model A tourer body for sale for NZ$9250.00 and appeared to only have minimal rust. You don't find them this complete or in such good condition very often these days.

MAIN: Bare metal '30 Ford coupe shares display space with the Kruzin Kustoms sponsored Nigel Dixon Top Doorslammer Falcon that is chasing the title to become NZ's first five second doorslammer. The chopped coupe is flathead Ford V8 powered with twin Stromberg 97 carbies.

ABOVE: Mid West Street Rods were one of the many clubs on display camping at Kumeu for the weekend with this great lineup of members cars. Left to right we have '42 Chevy fleetline fastback sedan, '39 Ford beer barrel pickup, '35 Ford five window coupe and '36 Ford five window coupe. Take your pick!

LEFT: The talented air brush artists were popular again with crowds around them all weekend.

ABOVE: Jim Hanham's '34 Ford roadster was first rodded in the fifties and it's completely legal in its "as is" state with natural patina.

ABOVE RIGHT: For NZ$40,000.00 you could have driven home in Murray Frank's Model T coupe. It is 327 Chevy powered with Turbo 350 transmission and is a real blast from the past.

RIGHT: Casey Hill has done it all with the ex Bill Ward Model A Bonneville roadster now running a Honda V6 for power. Check out the Hemi powered, chopped '30 Model A coupe in the background too.

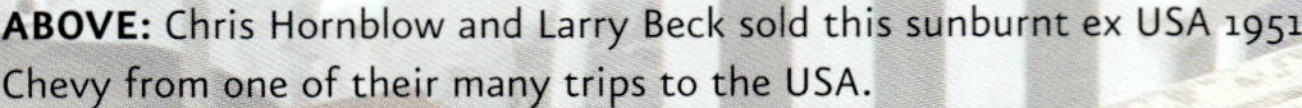

ABOVE: Chris Hornblow and Larry Beck sold this sunburnt ex USA 1951 Chevy from one of their many trips to the USA.

ABOVE: Hardly recognisable now but Noel Sutherland's '32 Ford roadster was once Lenny Jones' channelled show car of the sixties and seventies.

ABOVE: Justin Logan's striking '39 Ford convertible looks great in yellow with wide whites and solids. The chopped top just adds to its desirability.

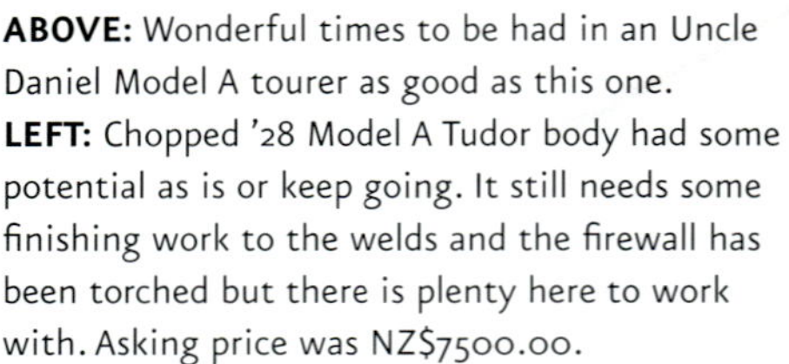

ABOVE: Wonderful times to be had in an Uncle Daniel Model A tourer as good as this one.
LEFT: Chopped '28 Model A Tudor body had some potential as is or keep going. It still needs some finishing work to the welds and the firewall has been torched but there is plenty here to work with. Asking price was NZ$7500.00.

ABOVE: Rex and Jenny Moyle are part of the retro caravan craze that hits New Zealand nationwide. The "Turkey Lounge" is their smartly dressed tear-drop trailer that follows behind their '57 Chevy tow car. Winner of Best Presentation award.

ABOVE RIGHT: Mark McAlpine was demonstrating his metal forming abilities while promoting his tech weekends.

BELOW: The swap meet area is vast and usually has some great parts and memorabilia like these toys. Collectors had plenty to pick from at this stand that was conveniently displayed on a car bonnet.

BOTTOM: For NZ$6000.00 this repaired Model A Closed Cab body was a deal.

ABOVE: There's always plenty to discover in the swap meet area at Kumeu. Need a grille anyone? Take your pick!

BELOW: The makings of a C-Cab Model T pickup could be had in the swap meet area. plus a Model A roadster street rod project.

ABOVE: A cheap way to go drag racing was this Hambster style dragster. The nostalgia style dragster is late model Falcon six cylinder powered and was for sale for NZ$4500.00. If you need more grunt there's a twin four equipped 327 Chevy engine in the foreground and a later model 350 Chevy on the far side.

ABOVE: Dark green '56 Ford F100 is a desirable parts hauler that remains left hand drive and has been dumped in the weeds. This one is owned by Steve White who recently put the truck on the road as his latest project. The "LOST-56" has gained a new life!

MAIN: Colin and Juliann Pearce have a striking combination in the form of this '57 Chev on chrome Rallye wheels and teardrop camper trailer.
ABOVE: Nikki Martin's '32 Ford roadster is a real lesson in period correct hot rodding with triple carbs, Offy heads and "V8 KID" plates. Sounds like fun.
ABOVE LEFT: Originally rodded in the eighties by John Hinton then Chris Walton, this Bonus pickup still looks all hot rod.
LEFT: There was an impressive array of custom motorcycles on display including this one with wild paint scheme.

Kumeu - New Zealand

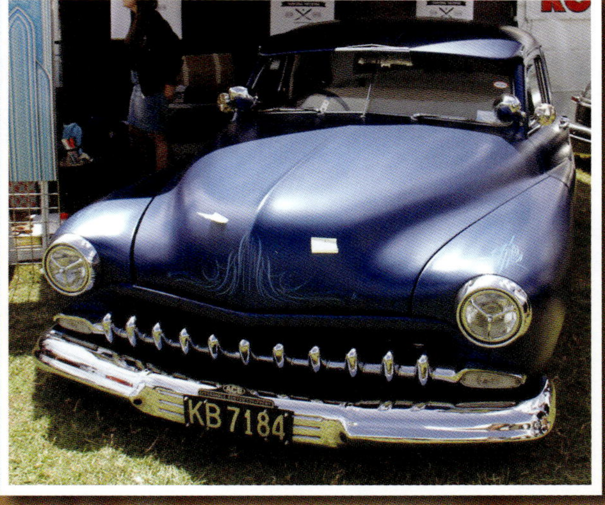

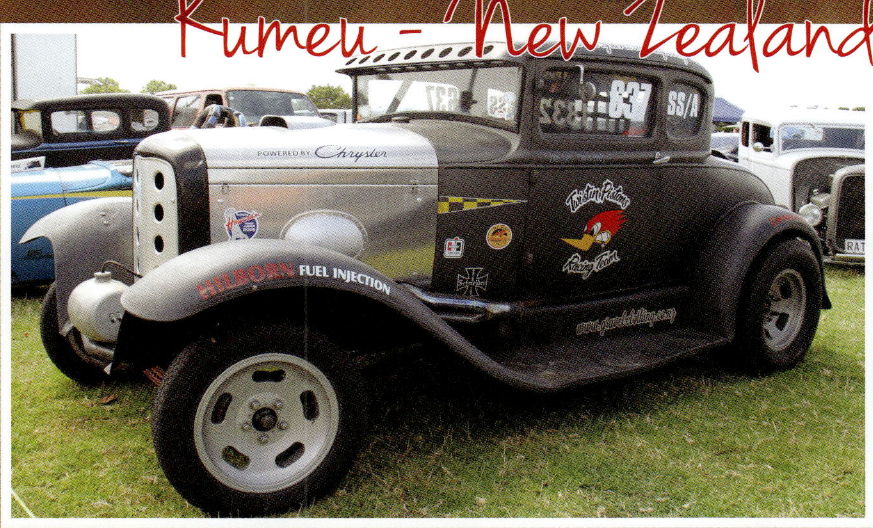

ABOVE: Charlie "Chaz" Allen was kept busy laying down some pinstriping on Paul Nicholl's bagged '51 Mercury.

ABOVE: Dave Best's gasser style Model A coupe is as cool as they come with a Hemi and four speed. The chopped Model A coupe is from the "Twistin' Pistons" racing club.

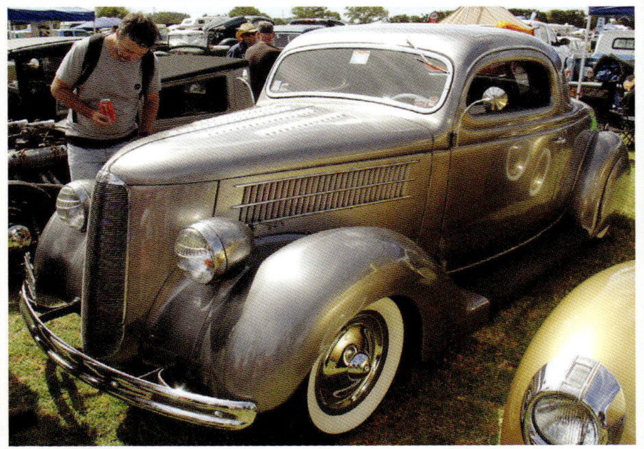

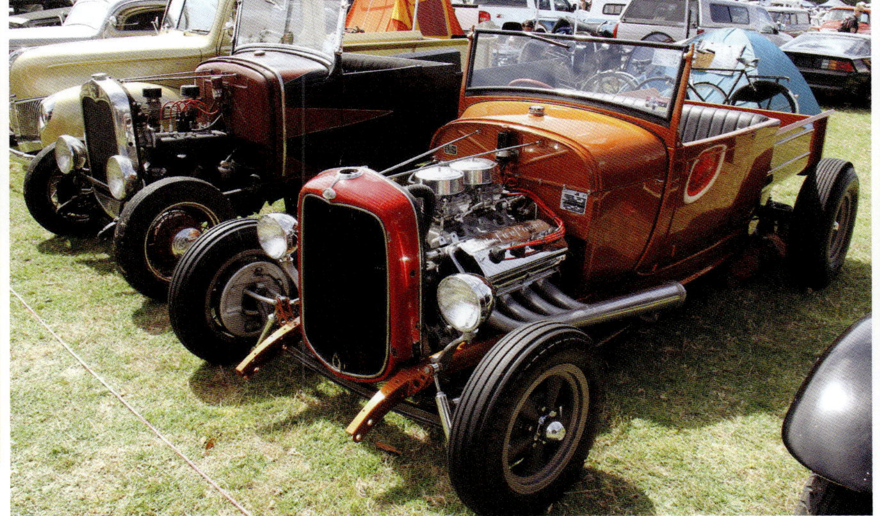

ABOVE: Tania Foster's '36 Ford coupe never fails to impress with a DeSoto Hemi and Calori coupe styling in bare metal.
RIGHT: Kirstin Courtney's and Roger Johnson's Model A pickups with four banger and Hemi power respectively.

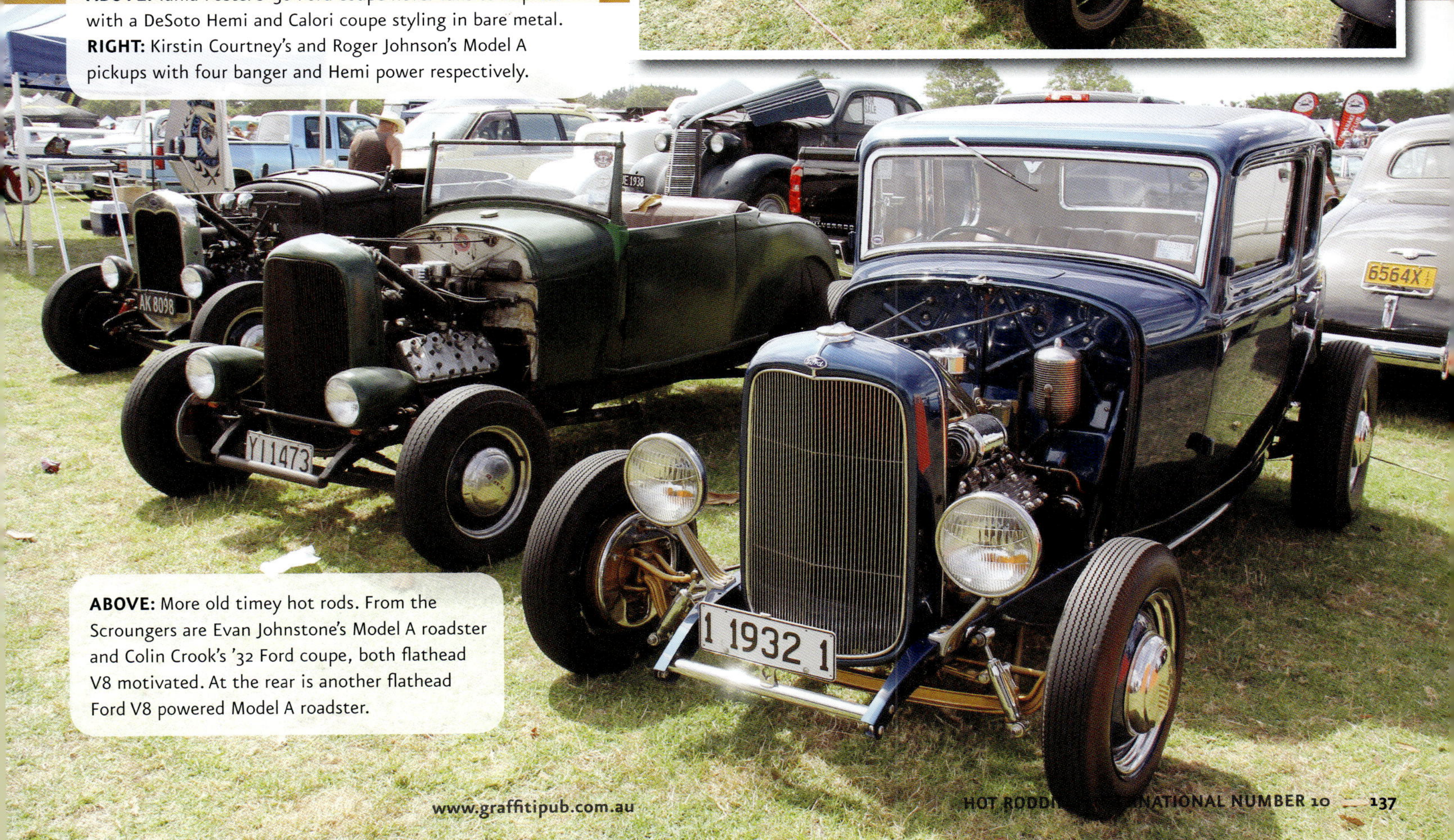

ABOVE: More old timey hot rods. From the Scroungers are Evan Johnstone's Model A roadster and Colin Crook's '32 Ford coupe, both flathead V8 motivated. At the rear is another flathead Ford V8 powered Model A roadster.

Lifelong Passion

PROFILE: Lenny Souter

I grew up on a market garden at Dingley, behind Pirotta's sand pits but didn't have much interaction with them. There were plenty of old cars around the area and I was given a '34 Vauxhall that still had the original curtains in it. Father had a Bedford truck with similar mechanicals so the running gear was familiar. My next car was a '28 Chevy that I bought from a neighbour who bought cars like this with rego on them, drove them until the rego ran out and then parked them.

While still in tech school I paid £75.0.0 for a '34 Ford coupe from a guy named Clark, it had been put off the road by the police as unroadworthy. I was too young to drive it home so I got a mate to drive it. I then scoured the little books for articles on channelling, did it by the book and the car still exists today, but has been put back up on top of the chassis.

At school I learnt to use oxy/acetylene welding equipment and taught myself to arc weld. I went full bore on building the '34 coupe using the little magazines as my inspiration. From the magazines it was obvious OHV engines were the way to go. Having sold the '34 in 1967 to Graham South and bought a Pontiac 347 engine from the Mercedes dealer in Frankston for £45.00 I made a bellhousing to fit a '39 Ford gearbox, plus the overdrive from a Triumph that was dumped in a creek. This converted the '39 gearbox to open drive and it had two gear sticks through the floor.

The first time I drove it at the drags in my deeply channelled Model A tourer I raced a gold GT Falcon police car and beat it. The first GTs were only available in gold and even the police version was gold. I would take off in second gear and only use second and top with an ET of 14 seconds @ 104 mph. It would smoke the tyres with ease. Those tyres came off Charlie

**Words & Photos: Larry O'Toole
and Lenny Souter Collection**

ABOVE: Model T roadster with Deuce grille and chassis and four banger driveline is Len's latest project.
BELOW LEFT: Rare '32 Chevy five passenger coupe "Vicky" awaits its turn for a rebuild. Len has been considering selling the car but likes it too much to be serious about moving it on.
BELOW: Running Model A roadster ute is an all original item amongst Len's vast collection.

Pirotta's Imperial that the local tyre service took off when they still had reasonable tread on them. They were 26 inches tall. The diff was a '53 Cusso that was unbolted from a dumped wreck. I bent the diff at the drags and it split at the back, dripping oil out, so I pulled it out and jacked it straight again. The car was so heavily channelled that girls' short skirts were above the top of the door level. I welded domes on the pistons in the Pontiac engine while it was still in the car!

There were lots of hot rodders in the Dandenong area where Graham South lived. When I sold him the '34 Ford coupe it had a defence force flathead V8 in it that was later swapped for a 327 Rambler. Graham on-sold it to a guy at Cockatoo where it survived the bushfires by being towed into the clear at the local footy ground.

After the channelled Model A tourer I wanted a T Tudor, so I wrote to the USA seeking one. I got a T coupe body to replace the T Tourer body but it never happened and I am still driving the tourer now. The car ran a 283 Chevy with Studebaker bellhousing that allowed a Borg Warner three speed transmission from a Customline to bolt up. It ran 14.5 at the drags – was a good combination.

Chris and I took the tourer to the USA on our honeymoon. I knew some of the NorCal/Bay Area rodders from whom I bought a Model A flatback pickup and built it into a rod for my brother. Tony Di Benedetto later rebuilt this Model A into a show car.

I picked up a cheap '55 Chevy two door sedan from the head honcho at GM in Dandenong and gave it a quick rebuild over 14 weeks, before anyone else was bringing them into the country. I put a flip front on it. Picked up a cheap '29 six cylinder Chev sedan for which some uni students paid me good money. Then I

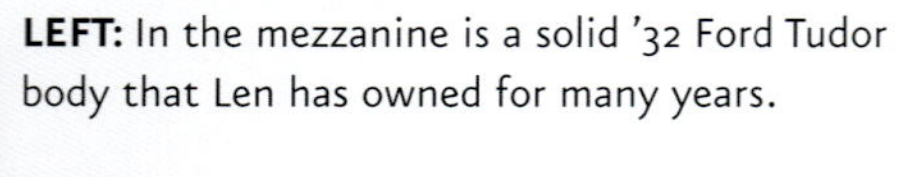

LEFT: In the mezzanine is a solid '32 Ford Tudor body that Len has owned for many years.

BELOW: That's an old flathead Cadillac engine sitting in a Deuce chassis.

BOTTOM: Garden art consists mostly of old Model A Ford wrecks that add real atmosphere to Len and Chris' rural property "Broken Downs" near Mansfield, Victoria.

built a T bucket with a 327 Chevy engine. Bought a blower from the USA but it made the T too powerful and I thought someone would kill themselves in it, so I pulled the engine and put the car up for sale. We moved to Baxter and sold up at Dingley in 1969. There was a whole bunch of young blokes in the area and they soon realised I was into rods. I was a Pegasus member but now too far away, so I asked the club to help me form Bay Rodders – there were lots of guys moving out from the inner city. Twenty-six people formed Bay Rodders at a meeting at the Baxter Community Hall where we met on the second Tuesday of each month. I had to be up early for market so I could get to the meetings that evening. They are still held on the same day each month and there are still eight foundation members active in the club. I believe wives and families need to be involved in clubs so they always have been in Bay Rodders.

It was not unusual to have 75 kids at the club's Christmas breakups where one year Santa appeared in a helicopter and all the kids became upset when he was water-bombed.

Car activity slowed down a bit as we concentrated on keeping the farm going but I did have a '56 Chevy hardtop and son, Dain wanted a car. I had a '32 chassis he could use and a '32 Ford roadster body hanging up since before we were married. He wanted that too but I said no, he could have a T roadster that I found under the trees at the Wantirna market site. The owner wanted $350.00 when I was only earning $75.00 a week and I couldn't afford it. The car was sold but the new owner only wanted the rolling chassis and left the body behind. I bought that for $50.00.

Dain wanted to use a 350 Chevy engine but I was wary that he would hurt himself so went with a P76 V8. He has been

www.graffitipub.com.au

TOP: The current "drivers" the T roadster, T tourer and '34 Ford coupe.
ABOVE LEFT: Flathead V8 in a rodded '32 Ford chassis is destined to go under a future project.
ABOVE RIGHT: Mint '32 Ford roadster body has been in Len's collection for years.

THIS PAGE: The '27 T roadster was purchased in the USA and updated to local specifications to suit our registration requirements in Australia. It has a Westcott fibreglass repro body painted Toreador Red metallic with tan leather interior and English square weave carpet. It is mounted on a '32 Ford chassis that has been pinched and boxed to suit the '27 T body. The engine is a '33 C model four banger of 210 cubic inches that has been fitted with a Riley Price overhead valve conversion and twin Dellorto side-draft carburettors. The manual transmission in the T roadster is from a '39 Ford but fitted with '48 Ford gears and the rear end is from a '40 Ford with finned brake drums fitted.

everywhere in that car, it is reliable and really nice to drive. All four of our children Karli, Dain, Braydon and Tarsha now have special cars of their own.

When growing up the kids had no options, the farm had us tied up so they had to go with us all the time. We always had baby seats in the rods and I recall the cops commenting on how we had the baby seats belted into the rods. They were trying to get the government to make it compulsory for ordinary cars and were surprised we rodders were already doing it.

These days we mostly get good respect from the police and there are very few bad rods any more. If they aren't up to spec they don't last long. They now have good brakes, good driving habits and it is a great culture where the people all relate to each other.

In 1977 we took the T tourer to the states on our honeymoon. I wrote to Gary Meadors at the NSRA before he started Goodguys. He was secretary of the NorCal Early Iron and handed the letter around. Members responded but I got the dates wrong, the event was one week earlier than I thought. We changed the plane tickets for no extra charge and moved the shipping forward. Then the ship caught fire in LA and was impounded. A friend of the owner talked them into moving the container with the T inside. The car was unloaded and had been driven around inside the shipping yard. The engine had

ABOVE: On the road the T is a lot of fun to drive and it has that distinct sound that four bangers with overhead valve conversions emit.

RIGHT: An appropriate property name for a retired hot rodder.

FAR RIGHT: Len's workshop is where dreams come true. Everything about it is old school style, even the secret door lock!

caught fire in it and the shipping people didn't want any more trouble, so they got us and the car out super quick.

We spent 36 hours behind the wheel, driving straight through from LA to meet up with the SFO gang along the way. There weren't any mobile phones in those days so they left phone messages at police stations along the route and we eventually caught up with them. It was to be a once in a lifetime honeymoon trip but in three years we were back there again in the ex-Wes Bennett '35 Ford ute. In four weeks we covered 6500 miles. The T had Jag rear etc. and some of the Americans thought my workmanship was a bit rough and ready, but we had no problems and I ended up helping all but one of

them with their own mechanical problems. We headed straight across to Minnesota from California and came back via Montana where we encountered mountains twice as high as we have in Australia – it was very cold, even in mid-summer. We were taken with the massive peaks and took lots of amazing pictures. The people were all fantastic and the hospitality first class.

I had been to the USA once previous to this, for a trade show, and we still stay in touch with friends over there all the time. They are generally very ignorant of Australia but it's not their fault, they are just not exposed to the rest of the world outside America. We get worldwide news, they mainly only see American news. They have a naïve idea of what Australia is

ABOVE: One of Len's first hot rods was this channelled '34 Ford coupe.
LEFT: A much younger bare-chested Len with his '27 T tourer at a rod run in the USA. Note the RHD sign on the rear of the tourer. Len and wife, Chris took the T to the USA on their honeymoon.
BELOW LEFT: Len bought this '35 Ford ute from Wes Bennett, drove it around while in the USA and sold it to a new American owner who still has it today.
BELOW RIGHT: Len and Chris spent their honeymoon touring the USA in the '27 T tourer. They were the first Aussie hot rodders to complete such an exercise.

like, some even asked if we had washing machines!

The second trip was to the Nationals in Memphis TN and we went to New Orleans etc., while there. We are still in contact with people from this 1980 trip too. The ute is still going, it has new paint but is otherwise the same as when we took it over and sold it there. It still has the 283 Chevy engine, Holden front end and manual Powerglide transmission that Wes Bennett fitted when he built it. The Americans couldn't believe that the lambswool seat covers wouldn't be hot to sit on. We had baby Karli with us and she was in a lambswool lined baby seat, they were astounded! We Aussies have a gifted life, we can do anything we like but in other places in the world that's just not possible.

The '35 ute went into San Francisco, from there we crossed lower down to Texas and back into So-Cal. When pulled up for a passport check the police wanted to know all about Australia.

Chris and I are now retired, we sold out of the market garden after 1995 as the children weren't interested in continuing on with it and we started looking for another business. We looked at supermarkets etc., but all were too hard. Eventually we purchased the Mansfield Caravan Park. It was good to move away from the urban area where you didn't have to worry about your family being exposed to drugs etc., a much better environment for the kids to grow up. I'm not sorry we did the market gardening, but selling it was a great move at the right time. Mansfield is a progressive town with good people and basically only two seasons, in summer everyone flocks to nearby Lake Eildon and in the winter they pass through on their way to the snow. There are a couple of active car clubs in the area plus charity groups so there is plenty going on. I always thought we would return to the Mornington Peninsula but that's not likely now, we're too busy enjoying retirement in Mansfield.

I am also into veteran motorcycles, all pre-1920, something I inherited from my father as he had such bikes all his life. I find the bike fraternity are an older age group.

Rodding has now moved along considerably thanks to the availability of new repro parts that are unique to rodding. Whole new sheet metal repro cars are now available in rodding but it's not the same for the restorers.

My latest project is a T roadster with Riley overhead conversion on the four-banger engine. I bought it out of the USA six years ago when I went over with Dain. We had been to the Street Rod Nationals and were on our way to Bonneville via a Goodguys run in Spokane, Washington. One guy went off and found a yard full of cars and the four port Riley equipped roadster was among them. It was cheap enough but the owner was dubious about selling. He suffered a bout of ill health and

ABOVE: Yard art takes many forms at "Broken Downs" but most of it is old Model A bits and pieces including this partially rodded roadster with front and rear ends lying nearby.

LEFT: Radically low was the channelled Model A tourer that Len built in the 1960s. It featured a Pontiac V8 engine and sporty upswept exhaust tips at the rear.

then offered it to me for a cheaper price. We went over for a wedding vow renewal ceremony and drove to Spokane to pick it up. The car sat in the USA for some time but the kids were all set up so I shipped it home and started work on it. These engines, when equipped with an overhead valve conversion, have a sound all of their own. I recently converted the roadster to RHD. I love the colour and the style of the interior trim, it's a lovely little car.

Youngest daughter Tarsha decided she would like a rod so I suggested we build the '32 roadster for her. No, she wanted a '34 Ford coupe right or wrong, so I contacted some friends in the US to see if they knew of one that might be for sale. We located one but it wasn't for sale – yet. Bill Mendosa, a friend of Jim Gomes owned the car and was still driving it. He indicated he might sell it in 10-12 months time as he needed some money to get the trim in a Caddy done. We stayed in contact and were sent a folder with photos and a firm price – no offers! I consider it was quite cheap, the guy had owned it for years and it only needed pulling apart and tidying up. It's a nice car to drive and has 350/Turbo 400 running gear. It consists of a steel body with fibreglass fenders and came from Sacamento in California. Tarsha is the youngest and is quite petite, so I had to make sure there was plenty of adjustment in the seat so she could drive the car. She loves the car, but for

some reason it always comes home with no fuel in the tank!

I have helped all of our kids get into a car and for Karli that meant a nice '35 Ford Tudor. I was building them a '32 Tudor but it was taking too long, so thought maybe we could pick up something while our grandchild was still young. I found the '35 Tudor here in Australia where it had been for six years. It was on H plates so I test drove it and decided it was the right car for her. I set about making it more user friendly. I pulled the front off it and converted it to RHD. It does everything right, just check the oil and go. Karli and Daniel live in Wodonga and Daniel has very good knowledge of the car that had a Mustang II front end that needed some attention. It was corrected and converted back to manual steering. Nothing needed major surgery, just a tidy up and make it more serviceable. It has Chevy 350/350 and a S10 rear end. The tailshaft angles needed correcting. I didn't try to screw the previous owner down on price, Karli and Daniel have two small children so it was very suitable for them. They tow a trailer with it and it is set up properly to suit that purpose.

Other son, Brayden is into a different style of car and has his own DeLorean.

In the shed at home is another project, a widened and lengthened Model A flat back pickup that is being built on a truck chassis. It is nicely balanced and eventually I intend to

LEFT: Early Model A closed cab pickup is one of Len's "next" projects. It will feature a widened cabin that makes use of reproduction rear and side panels. The side panels are also longer than standard to give more leg room inside the cabin. The sun visor is also a custom made piece to suit the wider cabin. Note that even though the cabin is wider, the cowl remains standard Model A. The pickup is being built on a Model AA truck chassis.

RIGHT: The rear of cabin panels have been widened as shown in the photo. Additional widening strips have been inserted down the length of each leading door pillar so it is hard to pick unless you know Model As. This is what allows the cowl section to remain standard.

LEFT: A steel original dash from a '35 Ford has been modified at the ends to fit the widened Model A cabin to give it a unique custom style inside as well.

use it to carry my little T roadster to long distance rod runs. It will be partly enclosed, so we can use it as a terrace at rod runs in the future.

Hanging in the roof is the '32 Ford roadster that used to belong to Ken Smith of the Pegasus club. He was going to build it for himself, but with three children including a set of twins, it wasn't going to be practical. I talked him into trading me the roadster for a Model A Tudor, but then I couldn't find one that was suitable. I did locate a '32 Ford sedan, so I offered to trade that for the roadster and did the deal three weeks before we were married. Chris, my soon to be wife didn't object, she has been supportive of my car hobby all the way through our married life. The roadster body is still hanging in the shed roof all these years later, but I have accumulated everything else required to build the car. I once would have put a strong motor in it, but now that I am older I am leaning toward sidevalve running gear with all the correct period stuff.

The '32 Chevy five passenger (Vicky) I have toyed with selling but I'm not sure I really want to get rid of it. I would like to build it myself.

I did a little bit of drag racing but mostly only at a local level. The guys deeply into it always seemed to be a day and a dollar short and I could see it was too expensive for me to keep up. I did enjoy competing at the low level I could afford though.

I have always taken an interest in salt lake racing and bought all the bits to build a car for the purpose. I had a Formula 5000 engine that I bought from Graham McRae already fully rebuilt. I reckoned on putting it into a Model A tourer with all the trick stuff and after my first trip to the salt I thought, "We can do this!" Why not have a 200 mph street rod?

I worked with the Rea/Weir/Mumford team for a few years when they were racing their T roadster, but they decided not to continue so I got involved with scrutineering. An American friend came out and did an article on the trip to the Australian salt lake racing and back, with a few days in Adelaide spliced into the trip as well. We stayed back and helped pack up after the meeting where too much of the work was left to too few people. The article stirred quite a bit of interest in the USA and led to the visit by the American teams that came out in 1995 under Dick Williams' organisation. I would have liked to have helped more, but my own work regime didn't allow me time. The American interest has remained in our salt lake racing and especially now that they have been having some problems getting a suitable racing

ABOVE & LEFT: Len is also into veteran motorcycles, all pre-1920, something he inherited from his father as he had veteran bikes all his life. In the foreground is a four cylinder Ace that when brand new was twice the price of a Model T Ford car. Behind the Ace in the picture above is a 1913 Sun with Precision engine. They were Healey built with the same insignia design on the fuel tank as the Herald Sun newspaper used years ago when it was known only as "The Sun".

ABOVE: FN four cylinder – lots were sold in Australia by Fabere National. FN Rifles were from the same company.

ABOVE: Harley flat twin 1919, only made for a couple of years, this one is the first year model and came without a headlight.

ABOVE: Peugeot WWI despatch riders' bike, made from 1914-1917 and the only one in Australia. Len's dad started restoration on board the ship on the way to Australia.

surface at Bonneville. Only outside interests could cause problems here, the salt itself is in no danger of deterioration like has happened at Bonneville.

I am one of five life members of Bay Rodders, one of the nicest things that has happened to me. It was quite unexpected. I was president five or six times, but couldn't do it now. It is time for the younger brigade to take over and that is how it should be. I still attend Bay Rodders meetings even though we have remained in the Mansfield area.

Nobody was making anything to dress up Jag rear ends when I first built my T tourer so I had some tie bars cast in gun metal. Quite a few ended up on Bay Rodders' cars. I knew a pattern maker so I had Jag rear covers made too, with Souter cast into them. There were about 30 or 40 cast and it is amazing how many are still around. I had them made so the name could be taken off but nearly all left it in place. The diff cover was a two piece pattern.

I am finding many of my old friends that were involved in hot rodding in the early days are getting back into the hobby in their retirement. Some of them I haven't seen for years and it is great getting together again.

I also did some "GM Power Ahead" plaques with four or five different castings. I also did some rocker covers and there is a set on Dain's T roadster today. They have "Hot Wheels" cast into them and I have still got the pattern. I never intended to make them into a business, just did them so I could have something different. My brother made the short water pump drive systems for small block Ford Windsors, they used a six cylinder Holden water pump. I have always taken the attitude of seeing a problem and setting about fixing it.

I have never been big into car shows but always took part as a club exercise and the club won Top Display a few times. The members came up with some good ideas over the years including the use of a smoke machine for a drag racing theme with car lifters that made it look like they were doing wheelstands. One year we put Brian Kenyon's car up on a birthday cake, it all worked good, mounted on a turntable off a truck. Shows are always a lot of work and these days there are many really nice cars. I would like to see a display of three or four cars from 30-40 years ago that are still around. The average person can't afford to build top end show cars but it can still be done on a budget, especially if done by a young and old person combination. There is so much to pick from now in the way of engines, paint etc. It can be done to a high standard of finish over a time period. In my experience the older rodders will help in this regard if they are approached properly. ■

TOP END RUMBLE

For participants in a long distance rod run like the Top End Rumble, just as much enjoyment is gained from the trip there and back as from the event itself.

For us the adventure began when we left Castlemaine on Wednesday May 31 in two vehicles, our work station wagon and the XP 1000 Falcon van, all loaded with the show stand materials for the Queensland Hot Rod and Street Machine Spectacular, plus everything we needed to travel to Darwin and back in the van. The trip to Brisbane was uneventful and proceeded without a hitch apart from the normal delays experienced between Coffs Harbour and the Queensland border due to the ongoing roadworks that see much of this section restricted to 80 kph. Thankfully, much of it will soon be completed. Along the way we made overnight stops in Sydney, and Ballina, arriving in Brisbane at midday on the Friday, our appointed time to set up for the show.

The Queensland show was another success with good crowds for both days and a great cross-section of vehicles on display. We made contact with several NSW rodders who were also heading for Darwin and taking in the Queensland show on their way. While Al stayed in Queensland and returned directly to Castlemaine in the work wagon, Mary and I continued on north straight after the show with stops at Nambour for lunch with Steve Hadlow and Hervey Bay overnight.

We also took the opportunity to check out the Maryborough Showgrounds where the 2019 ASRF Street Rod Nationals will be staged. It looks eminently suitable with good facilities and plenty of serviced camping space.

We both awoke during the night with severe headaches, a portent of what was to come with both of us suffering heavy colds over the next few days. Next stop was Rockhampton where we caught up with Warren Burggraaff and checked out the projects in his workshop. We also made a quick trip to Yeppoon to shoot a car feature and returned to Rockhampton where Warren gave us a quick guided tour of the city.

ABOVE L to R: Ready to leave from outside the Graffiti office in Castlemaine, Queensland Hot Rod Show bound and then on to Darwin. Wildlife encountered in central Queensland included a mob of emus. A social call at Steve Hadlow's in Nambour to check out his latest projects after completing his Model A roadster pickup.

BELOW L to R: Emerald hot rodder Alwyn Davis still has the custom FX Holden ute he built with turbocharged red motor in the 1990s. Short work is made of road kill kangaroos by the wedge-tailed eagles. A stop in Maryborough, Queensland to check out the site for the 2019 ASRF Street Rod Nationals.

Road Trip
An epic rod run

Words & Photos: Larry O'Toole

ABOVE: Freight movement in outback Australia is big business and it uses big vehicles. Typical are these road trains with four trailers and over 80 wheels. Encountering one of these on the road requires alert driving as overtaking can be a long process, you need plenty of clear road ahead.

ABOVE: The XP delivery is dwarfed by a Qantas jumbo jet at the Qantas Founders Museum in Longreach, Queensland, a fascinating place to gain an appreciation of Australia's air transport history.
BELOW: The shearers' memorial in Barcaldine highlights the birthplace of the Australian Labour Party. Warning signs alert drivers to the special requirements when encountering road trains. The crossroads of Australia is where the north-south Stuart Highway meets the Barkly Highway at Three Ways in the Northern Territory.

to Darwin and back

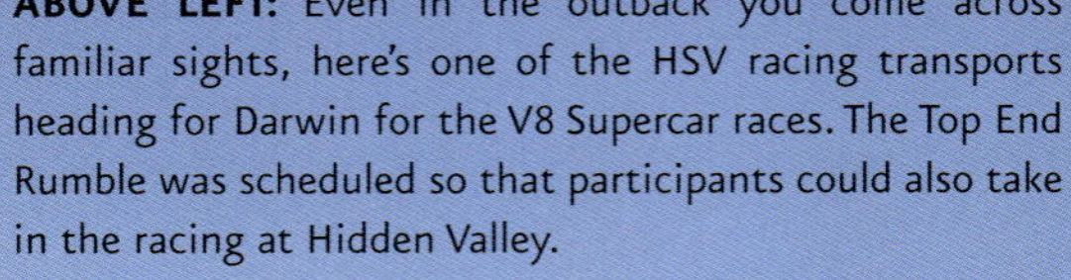

ABOVE LEFT: Even in the outback you come across familiar sights, here's one of the HSV racing transports heading for Darwin for the V8 Supercar races. The Top End Rumble was scheduled so that participants could also take in the racing at Hidden Valley.

ABOVE: Everyone travelling to the top end has to make a stop at the famous Daly Waters pub. You won't find a more typical outback pub with years of memorabilia pinned up everywhere inside, including currency from all around the world. The pub was rumoured to have been sold recently for $7 million!

LEFT: Julie Loomes decided she was going to Darwin no matter what and drove all the way from Bendigo in central Victoria with husband, Mick in the passenger seat of her V6 Buick powered Model A coupe.

MAIN: Time for a memorable photo opportunity on reaching the Northern Territory border. Mary and I shared the driving all the way up and back.

Next morning we headed for Longreach with a stop at Emerald to check out Alwyn Davis' immaculate '34 Chevy two door sedan. Alwyn and fellow local, Ian McCallum ('34 Chev roadster) were preparing to join us on the way to Darwin but leaving a couple of days later. We stayed two nights in Longreach to give us time to see the Stockman's Hall of Fame and the Qantas Founders Museum. Of note through this area was the amount of road kill, easily the most we saw for the whole trip, mostly dead kangaroos, plus the eagles and hawks that feast on the carcasses.

Next stop was Mt Isa, again for two nights to enable us to learn some of the history of the copper and lead mining that has been carried on there since the 1920s. Unfortunately it seems the mining operations might have a limited future, which will be devastating for the town. Whilst in Mt Isa we saw another NSW rod heading for Darwin, a '34 Chevy coupe.

From Mt Isa we headed for Barkly Homestead, which was to be our major fuel and lunch stop for the day. Our target was to reach Three Ways as our overnight stay and we arrived fairly early. Alwyn and Dyrelle Davis and Ian McCallum caught up to us there and we played tag with them all the way to Katherine where all

TOP: You knew gassers towed caravans didn't you? Chris Hadgkiss drives his '40 Willys all over the place, including to Darwin and back!

ABOVE: Zipping along the highway in the Northern Territory is Geelong Street Rodder, Rob Astill in his '33 Chevy coupe, also with caravan in tow.

BELOW: This is exactly what Ian Hickey had in mind when he built his '37 Ford pickup (with '35 grille). The ideal vehicle for pulling a caravan all over Australia.

BOTTOM: Ralph Harding's bright red Compact Fairlane looks outstanding, even in towing mode.

ABOVE RIGHT - TOP TO BOTTOM: Max Green made the round trip in quick fashion in his '47 Ford sedan. Blown big block power provides ample pulling power for Alan White's '34 Chevy two door sedan. Unfortunate accident near Darwin involved a truck with giant video screen attached that was headed for the Supercar races — not a pretty picture. Alwyn Davis at speed in his superb '34 Chevy two door sedan that features LS 1 Chevy power out of a Holden Statesman.

ABOVE: Greg Smith made it to Darwin in his '41 Ford pickup with caravan in tow but suffered engine problems that ultimately led to an engine swap at Alice Springs on the way home to Geelong. He made it home ...eventually!

ABOVE: Believe the signs! There are crocodiles in the northern waterways and you need to believe the local authorities. Some places you can swim, some your dare not.

ABOVE: Peter and Jeanette Gregory take their '34 Ford tourer everywhere and tow their teardrop camper most of the time as well, so heading from Melbourne to the top end was just another rod run for them.

ABOVE: Ian McCallum finished his '34 Chev roadster just a few weeks before the Top End Rumble and drove it on its maiden voyage from Emerald in Queensland. The purple roadster performed flawlessly all the way.

BELOW: Fuel stop for Mick Fitzpatrick in the yellow '34 Chevy roadster and John Viles in the '49 Ford woody delivery. Both travelled from the NSW Central Coast to be part of the Top End Rumble. Inset is a photo of some vintage tin beside the Hayes Creek service station, a sure-fire lure to get hot rodders to stop. The Sloper body appears to be an Oldsmobile or Pontiac, too far gone to rescue.

ABOVE: The Top End Rumblers were guests at the Mindil Markets in Darwin with a separate area set aside for a simple show and shine. In the foreground is Bruce Borlase's F1 Ford pickup from Melbourne with Wayne and Dianne Lockhart's '32 Ford five window coupe to the left. The Lockharts drove all the way from Launceston in Tasmania to take out the longest distance trophy and they did it with teardrop camper in tow.

LEFT: The rodders were honoured with a civic reception at the NT Parliament house on arrival in Darwin. Sitting outside here is John and Jean Wilson's Model A roadster. They were the main organisers of the Top End Rumble.

BELOW: One of the popular features of the Top End Rumble was for entrants to put their cars on display at the V8 Supercar races at Hidden Valley. Public attending the races had to walk from the car park right past the display of hot rods and customs as they entered the race track. The Top End Rumblers attracted lots of attention as a result.

participants were congregating for the final charge into Darwin. Most arrived in Katherine at least a day early to allow some time to rest up and take in a few of the local tourist attractions. For us that meant a trip up the Katherine Gorges in flat bottom boats where we saw crocodiles and the amazing sheer-walled river gorges. We highly recommend seeing this attraction if you ever get the chance.

Everyone was up early for breakfast at the showgrounds before heading off for Darwin after a pass through the main street of Katherine. Morning tea (and free entertainment from the proprietor) was at Emerald Springs with coffee, scones and delicious muffins on the menu. There were about 30 entries in the Darwin convoy and they looked fantastic scooting up the highway. We took the opportunity to start near the back of the pack and slowly overtake them to take photos on the move. Everyone reassembled at the Livingstone World War II air strip beside the highway for a group photo shoot from a cherry picker before driving the final few kilometres into the headquarters in Darwin, the Club Tropical Resort and neighbouring caravan park. Everyone made it with relatively few encountering problems along the way. The main issues were; broken coil-over shocker, excessive oil consumption, flat tyre and wheel bearing failures with most being attended to as soon as we arrived.

Jean Wilson and her committee had done a great job of organising the Rumble with one non-compulsory organised activity each day and plenty of time left for the southerners to check out all of Darwin and surrounding area's tourist attractions. The organised functions included a civic reception at Parliament

ABOVE: Participants assembled in Katherine for the final run into Darwin and then gathered again on the World War II Livingstone air strip for a photo opportunity before setting off on the final few kilometres into Darwin.

ABOVE: Ian Hickey tries his balancing ability on the rod balance, part of a day of driving event activities during the 10-day long Rumble.

BELOW: Rodders couldn't resist a picture with the old DC-3 on display in the outdoors section of the Aviation Museum. On the left is Chris Hadgkiss' '40 Willys coupe, in the centre is Peter Lauder's '56 F100 pickup and at the far side is Alan White's '34 Chevy two door sedan.

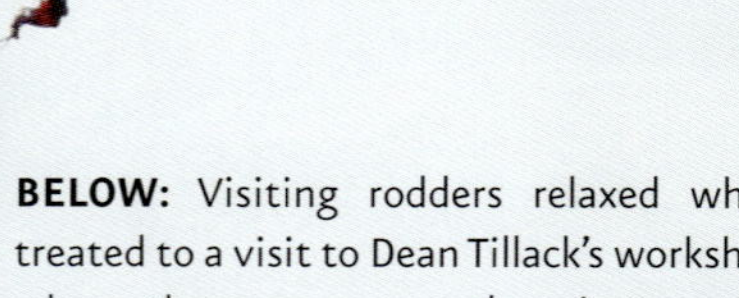

BELOW: Visiting rodders relaxed when treated to a visit to Dean Tillack's workshop where there were several projects under way and cool drinks in the Esky.

www.graffitipub.com.au

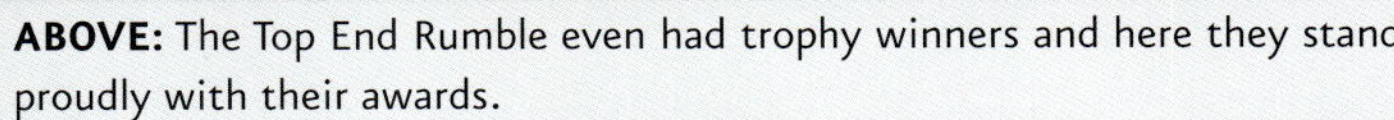

ABOVE: The Top End Rumble even had trophy winners and here they stand proudly with their awards.
LEFT: The open cars were invited to ferry the V8 Supercar drivers around the Hidden Valley circuit prior to the big race. In front is Ian McCallum's '34 Chevy roadster, next is Peter Gregory in the '34 Ford tourer and at the rear is Mick Fitzpatrick's yellow '34 Chevy roadster.

BELOW: Top eliminator at the rocker cover racing was Chris Hadgkiss, shown demonstrating that his win was thanks to sheer body strength ...oh and with a little help from some secret fuel ingredient as shown in the inset photo.

House on arrival in the northern capital, up to three days at the V8 Supercar races at Hidden Valley, where the open rods were invited to ferry drivers on a parade lap, visits to Mindil and Palmerston Markets, grass driving events and an outdoor movie night, an evening cruise into Darwin CBD and a visit to the Aircraft Museum.

Most of the entrants took in the main tourist attractions that included visits to wetlands to see crocodiles and other tropical beasties in the wild, the excellent Flying Doctor and World War II Bombing Museum on the main wharf, tours to the waterfalls of Litchfield National Park, plus several other attractions. Most were enjoying themselves so much they were thoroughly worn out at the end of each day from having such a good time.

Members of the Rumble group were also invited to visit a local rodder's workshop where several projects were under way. It was interesting to watch everyone relax in the familiar surrounds of a hot rod workshop like their own. Our thanks to Dean Tillack for making this generous offer and to Peter Brockwell for organising it.

The Top End Rumble ended on Friday June 23 with a dinner beside the pool at the Club Tropical Resort where everyone was in good humour, having made the most of the first organised rod run to the top end. A few trophies were presented to entrants and a presentation was made to Jean Wilson and her committee, for her fine effort in organising the event with assistance from husband John, brother-in-law Willie and son Adam.

ABOVE: Willy Wilson, John Wilson and Jean Wilson smile proudly after being presented with a gift of appreciation from the entrants of the Top End Rumble.

ABOVE: Termite mounds like these in Litchfield National Park are scattered over a wide area of the top end.

TOP: A stop at the War Cemetery at Adelaide River is a must for anyone travelling the Stuart Highway to or from Darwin.
ABOVE: The historic telegraph station at Tennant Creek.

ABOVE: Water tanks to aid drovers and stock movement were installed throughout the outback in the late 19th century and some have survived to today.

RIGHT: It's a long way to anywhere in Central Australia.

BELOW: Today outback travellers can make use of much more modern conveniences such as this service centre at Kulgera, south of Alice Springs.

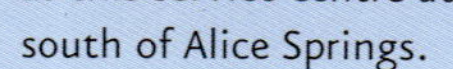

ABOVE & BELOW: Vintage tin is used in many places along the Stuart Highway to attract travellers to service centres. The line up above is at the Devils Marbles Hotel in the Northern Territory while the FJ Holden below is at Banka Banka Station.

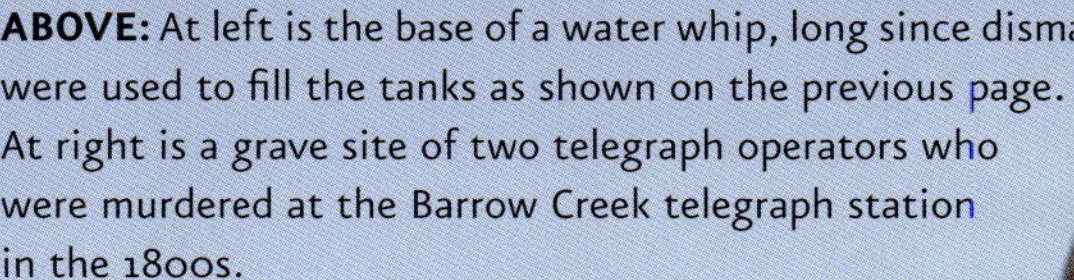

ABOVE: At left is the base of a water whip, long since dismantled. They were used to fill the tanks as shown on the previous page. At right is a grave site of two telegraph operators who were murdered at the Barrow Creek telegraph station in the 1800s.

The dinner on the final night of the Top End Rumble was a great way to end 10 days of activity and to talk about the trip back home. Most participants left the next morning and headed south, although a few stayed on for some more holiday time. We had pre-booked to be at Uluru for three days from June 27 so we had four days to get there from Darwin. That meant we didn't need to do huge days of travel but we did need to be conscious of how far we needed to travel each day. First stop out of Darwin was at Adelaide River for a look at the War Cemetery. After learning so much we never knew about the bombing of Darwin during World War II the cemetery held much more meaning as all of those killed during those bombing raids are buried at Adelaide River. The cemetery is beautifully kept and a fitting tribute to the sacrifice made by these people.

We continued on to Mataranka for our first overnight stay, at Bitter Springs just outside the township. First thing next morning we headed off with Tennant Creek as our proposed destination for that night. Along the way we stopped in at Daly Waters for morning tea where we met up with the Lockharts and Loomes' who were also Top End Rumblers on their way home. We would cross paths with them several more times as we travelled down the Stuart Highway. We made a few stops along the way to Tennant Creek to take in such sites as the Devil's Marbles, Barrow Creek and Tennant Creek Telegraph Offices. We were surprised to see how extensive the Devil's Marbles are and impressed that nobody has defaced them with graffiti.

From Tennant Creek we drove to Alice Springs, again with a few stops along the way, arriving in Alice Springs about 5:00 pm. We had been to Alice Springs before so it was only to be an overnight stop on this occasion, but still there was time to enjoy dinner at the Casino with local rodder Peter Templeton who had assisted several Top End Rumblers on their trip up to Darwin and would do it again for some on their way home. It's only about 450 km from Alice Springs to Uluru so we were able to have a relatively easy trip out there with a few stops along the way. Surprisingly we drove the last part of the day in rain, the first we had encountered since we left home. Maybe we would see it raining on the rock!

The rain stopped before we got to Yulara and we checked into our accommodation, did some shopping and enjoyed our first

FAR LEFT: Our stop at Barrow Creek attracted the attention of local, Leroy Hocking who recalled reading about XP 1000 back in 1982. He couldn't believe it was the same vehicle all these years later.
LEFT: It wasn't quite raining on the rock but it was on the way in. There was some water still trickling down its gullies when we got there.

MAIN: Spectacular is the only way to describe Uluru at sunset.
RIGHT: Relics of the rocket era adorn a local park beside the tourist information centre in the township of Woomera.
BELOW: The opal fields at Coober Pedy stretch for miles and appear almost as a moonscape due to most of the local housing being underground. There are so many holes in the ground that warning signs alert visitors of the danger.
BELOW RIGHT: "Mobile" apartments at the rear of the hotel in Melrose, South Australia.

TOP: Geographical features like this bluff abound in the top end as does wildlife like the beautiful wedge-tailed eagle.

glimpse of Uluru from a lookout in the resort property as daylight faded. It looked quite blue/purple as the sky was overcast and there wasn't any sunshine to provide a red sunset. Our first full day at Uluru we spent driving around the area scoping it all out and made a side trip to Kata Tjuta (the Olgas), west of Uluru. That took care of most of the day but we did decide that it would be worth going back the next day to walk up Walpa gorge at Kata Djuta and then return to Uluru to hire bikes and ride around the base of the rock.

The walk up the gorge in the early morning was freezing cold and very windy so it certainly woke up the senses. It had warmed up a bit by the time we got back to Uluru, so it was quite pleasant for our bicycle ride around the base of the rock. This allowed us to check out the rock up close, including all the little gullies and gorges with their rock pools, birds and in some cases aboriginal rock paintings. We left Uluru on the third morning and headed for Kings Canyon where we did the walk along the bottom. The rim walk is apparently quite spectacular but you need to be very fit to do that and it takes several hours to complete, so we elected to look after our health and only do the gorge walk along the bottom of the canyon. We also walked in to Kathleen Springs a little way down the road from Kings Canyon and found it well worth the walk along man-made pathways with a beautiful pool at the end. By the end of the day we had made it back to Erldunda on the Stuart Highway, ready to head south once again.

It felt like we were on the home run when we left Erldunda

the next morning with only two more stops scheduled before we made it home. The first was at Coober Pedy where the only accommodation we could find was in an underground B&B, a new experience. It is incredible how many mine mounds there are in the Coober Pedy area and we had quite a conversation with a local miner at Marla the last major stop before Coober Pedy. He gave us some sample rock with some opal colour in it and described how they mine for the opals.

On the way from Coober Pedy back to the Adelaide area we stopped off at Woomera for a look around the old town where there are samples of many of the rockets and missiles that were tested there back in the forties, fifties and sixties. We intended to make it at least to Port Augusta that evening, further south if we could. We made good time so headed inland slightly from Port Augusta and south through Wilmington, Melrose, Gladstone and Clare, making it to Clare by nightfall, so we made that our last overnight stay.

From Clare we travelled across the top end of the Barossa Valley and down to Murray Bridge to join the highway to home via Tailem Bend, Nhill, Dimboola and St Arnaud, arriving back in Castlemaine late in the afternoon on Monday July 3 having been away for just over a month.

We enjoyed the trip immensely and saw many parts of this huge country that we hadn't been to before. Altogether we covered 7,700.00 miles and the old XP 1000 van never missed a beat for the whole trip.

TOP: The only damage XP 1000 suffered was a stone chip to the windscreen just before reaching Darwin. To prevent the damage from getting worse we had the local Novus windscreen repairer attend to it and he soon had us seeing clearly again.

ABOVE: Accommodation was in short supply at Coober Pedy so we opted to try out an underground bed and breakfast apartment. For people that normally live above the ground it was a different experience.

RIGHT: Several years ago I wrote this book about Charlie Heard taking three ladies on an extended tour from Victoria up through the centre of Australia to Darwin and back via Queensland in 1930. We did the trip in the reverse direction but were able to recognise many of the places that Charlie and the ladies visited on their trip in a Hudson tourer. It added great extra interest to our own outback adventure.

BELOW: Painted silos are a new phenomenon in the South Australian and Victorian Mallee. This one is at Coonalpyn in South Australia – almost home.

RIGHT: Final fuel stop on arriving back in Castlemaine after a journey of over 7000 miles. XP 1000 performed flawlessly for the whole trip.

Charlie's Pride

RAY CHARLTON'S PERFECT PAIR OF FORDS

It almost goes without saying that most of our very early Australian hot rodders became interested in the hobby when they were exposed to American hot rod magazines. One of those early hot rodders is Ray Charlton, almost an elder statesman of the movement now that he is getting on in years. But getting on in years doesn't mean getting out of the hobby for Ray, he is still building high quality, very driveable street rods.

When Ray moved to Victoria from country NSW, while still only a teenager, he found himself in the Technical Book and Magazine Company shop in Swanston Street, Melbourne where he purchased his first hot rod magazine. The first hot rod he saw was a '32 Ford Sport Coupe and it wasn't long before Ray had his first car, long before he held a licence, a '36 Ford sedan that soon lost its front fenders to become an instant hot rod. That was followed by a rare 34 Plymouth Sports Coupe that had some accident damage, but no matter, just pull the fenders and Ray had another instant hot rod. And so the pattern was set. Cars were bought and sold from home, sometimes wrecked and before long Ray was habitually circulating from car yard to car yard buying up unwanted trade-ins that usually had at least a few weeks rego left on them, saving him from ever having to pay registration himself. He kept upgrading to better and better cars, all the while using the proceeds to further the hot rodding addiction.

Ray bought his first '32 Ford in 1959, a roadster from a D Wifren, he can still remember the name of the previous owner! Next, from Selwyn Ray at the old army test ground near Romsey in 1962, came the black roadster that he still owns today. This is the car seen in the pictures within this article, fitted with an Ardun equipped engine bought from Roger Harrison of Mildura. The first '32 roadster was sold when Ray and Bev were married.

Like most early hot rodders, drag racing formed part of the interest and Ray started participating right at the end of the Pakenham era, then continued at Riverside. He blew up the '34 Ford coupe and thought it better to have a race only car, so he didn't have to thrash all night to get the car going again to drive to work. The replacement race vehicle was a Model A Ford based altered with six cylinder Holden engine. It was to be the only pure drag car Ray ever owned. It was sold when Riverside closed and drag racing interests moved to Calder. Ray ran the altered at the first Calder drag meeting for the new owner.

Since he first started in the hobby, Ray estimates he has probably owned about fifty 1932 Fords. Sedans and tourers were considered fodder for wrecking in those early days, even the odd Sport Coupe passed through his hands, but Ray thought they didn't look like what was considered hot rod material. In 1968 he got his hands on the five window coupe body you see here from John Norton, in exchange for a tourer. The coupe soon became Ray's favourite

car, replacing the channelled '32 roadster that many readers would remember he had for years through the sixties and early seventies. It was bought as an abandoned rocket that had been driven until it stopped. When he tracked the car down it had been parked down the side of a house with a deep gutter along the side of the road. The rumble seat lid off the roadster was being used as a bridge over the gutter! Ray took it home, had Bob Plowman panel beat it into shape and he then drove it everywhere, even raced it a lot at Calder where he just uncorked the headers, raced all day, then re-capped the headers and drove home.

Fast forward to today and Ray, now residing near Castlemaine in central Victoria, is still playing with his old cars. Indeed the reliable old five window coupe has just emerged from a complete rebuild, ready for another life of rod runs and fun with fellow rodders. What's more, now he has a comfortable '48 Ford convertible in the stable as well.

Ray Charlton
1948 Ford Convertible
Faraday, Victoria, AUSTRALIA

After spending most of his life involved in hot rodding, during which time he owned mostly '32 Fords, Ray Charlton decided it was time for something with more space and comfort to carry the aging body. That something would ideally be a vehicle that still fits the street rod theme, but with more internal space. It turned out to be a '48 Ford convertible that Ray purchased in Detroit, sight unseen, from a small castings manufacturer, but had it checked locally by an agent.

Circumstances beyond Ray's control meant it took 12 months to complete the transaction and have the car shipped to Australia, mainly due to the cold northern winter in that part of the USA. At first Ray was apprehensive; "What have I done? Bought a 60 year old convertible from Detroit where they put salt on the roads to melt the ice!"

As it turns out the convertible had been stored for several years in the old Studebaker factory, but security wasn't great at that site so it had suffered the loss of few parts due to pilfering. However most of the important parts were there, apart from the boot lid, but the previous owner managed to round up a replacement before the car was shipped.

When the convertible arrived in Australia it was a pleasant surprise for Ray as it turned out to be better than he expected. There were just a few minor patches of rust in the floor, but overall the car was in quite good restorable condition.

Convertibles like these are renowned for having a substantial chassis under them but Ray improved his even further by fully boxing it in the areas where the factory didn't. The comfort level of the finished vehicle is greatly enhanced by the use of a Jaguar XJ12 front suspension system that was swapped in with all fittings and rubber mounts intact. The Jag front end came from a left hand drive vehicle so the rack and pinion steering was swapped for a right hand drive version and upper shock absorber mounts were fabricated and welded to the top of the suspension towers.

At the rear Ray opted for a reliable eight inch Ford rear end that is mounted on semi-elliptic springs that came as an aftermarket kit from the USA. The rear end retains its drum brakes that work in combination with the Jag discs up front and a Ford master cylinder with aftermarket booster.

In the engine bay we find a 351 Windsor that has been reconditioned, fitted with a mild cam, balanced and had the heads cleaned up, all by Rod Rainford in Bendigo. The engine is topped with an Edelbrock 600 carby with Caddy style repro air cleaner and evacuated by a set of home made tube headers. The transmission is a C4 automatic that is engaged by an XT Falcon column mounted

shifter using an Aussie Falcon crossover linkage under the transmission.

When it came time to prepare the body Ray turned to local panel beating guru, Craig Green who repaired the rusted sections and generally straightened out the body ready for paint. In the process, holes were filled and an electric latching mechanism was fitted to the boot. This latch has an internal switch but can also be tripped from outside the vehicle if required. Hard to find curved glass H4 inserts are used in the headlights while the taillights use lead inserts in stock housings. Turn indicators are located in the stock park lights at the front and the rears are small but very bright LED aftermarket items.

To facilitate the interior trim Ray used aluminium sheet to make up the trim cards and lined the interior with sound deadening sheeting before Gavin Hill trimmed it all in brown leather. The convertible top is a kit from America that comes with everything required and just needs to be fitted to the individual vehicle. Green tinted glass is used in all of the openings but the windscreens were cut from an Acco truck screen so that its tinted band across the top is incorporated into the '48 windscreens.

The dash was converted to right hand drive by cutting up and reworking the original, which Ray did at home with the intention that it could be used as a pattern. However, Craig Green decided it would be easier to finish that dash properly rather than alter another.

Wheels are Vintique 8x15 and 6x15 fitted with '46 Ford hub caps and whitewall tyres. The steering wheel is an aftermarket item and all of the window winder handles and latches are new old stock items. Paintwork was laid on by Mick Whiteside at Parsons' Smash Repairs using Falcon bright red. All of the factory trim is stainless steel that has been restored and polished by Francis Paul of AutoBling in Braeside. Reproduction bumpers are fitted at front and rear and the fuel tank is a new plastic item from Tanks in the USA while the battery is located under the rear seat. ◼

Ray Charlton
1932 Ford Five Window Coupe
Faraday, Victoria, AUSTRALIA

Ray's '32 Ford five window coupe has a long history, indeed it has been on the Australian rodding scene since it was first completed as a street rod way back in 1973. Australian '32 Fords weren't made in the five window configuration so they were very rare at that stage. Ray swapped a '32 tourer body for the coupe body in 1968 and set about turning it into a state of the art (for the time) street rod. When it was finished in 1973 it emerged with a Holden front end and a 283 Chevy engine that came out of a stock but accident damaged '60 Chev sedan. As such it came with a heavy cast iron Powerglide automatic transmission but Ray swapped that out in favour of a four speed manual transmission. In this form the coupe provided many years of reliable service.

Four years ago the big rebuild started using a complete rolling replacement chassis that Ray built up while working for CAV Engineering back in the early 1980s, after he left his long-time job as a glass fitter and manager for O'Brien's Glass. After the stint at CAV, Ray became self-employed when he moved to the Castlemaine, Victoria region, the self-proclaimed Street Rod Centre of Australia. The new chassis features a set of fully boxed frame rails combined with a formed steel channel centre X member, a perfect platform for a modern street rod.

The front end now uses a dropped forged axle, CAV four bar system and a right hand drive Vega steering box that, despite being brand new, needed a total rebuild due to faults in its manufacture. Front brakes use Falcon rotors with Holden calipers. At the rear there is another eight inch Ford diff mounted on Viking coil-over shockers from McDonald Bros with four bar system and a panhard bar.

The Deuce coupe uses a 383 version of the small block Chevy with alloy heads, all machined and assembled by Rod Rainford in Bendigo. Sanderson cast headers were used as Ray says they bolt on and you have no more trouble with them. The engine is topped with a trio of 2GC carbies on an Edelbrock manifold. The radiator is an original '32 Ford item that was re-cored many years ago and continues to do sterling duty. Transmission is a Turbo 700R fitted with a constant pressure valve body and a Lokar shifter. Paul Rogers sorted the transmission after Ray experienced some initial problems with the first rebuild by another operator. As with the convertible, Ray called on Craig Green to prepare the bodywork before it was painted in Melbourne in a modern version of the original Indy Orange colour that has graced the body since 1973. Myles Johnson added the pinstriping to the outside of the coupe.

Once again Ray made up all of the interior panels in aluminium and Craig Green even made up a metal headliner for the coupe that has been painted by Ray's son Steven, who helped out extensively on both projects, and then Ryan Ford went to work with his striping brushes. The end result looks like it is smooth material with the pinstriping added. The rest of the interior trim features burgundy leather by Mark Swallow over bucket seats of unknown origin. An under-dash brake system is fitted with Falcon master cylinder and an aftermarket seven inch diameter booster. The roll bar that Ray fitted way back in the coupe's first life was retained and new seat belts from Neil Stamp complete the safety requirements. The coupe has always featured a boot rather than a rumble seat and it gets plenty of use, although Ray admits he has now prepared some interior panels for this area as well, mainly to separate off the battery that is mounted behind the front seats.

Finishing off the coupe is a set of repro bumpers, the rear one on shortened irons and the front one soon to get the same treatment. Ray intends making up a set of sixties style nerf bars so he can run either the bumpers or the nerfs depending on his mood at any particular time. Wheels are Vintique steelies, the fronts 5x15 wearing 175/35 tyres and the rears 8x15 with 235/75 radials. Under the rear of the body is a classy Caldwell stainless steel fuel tank that Ray has had for many years.

VICTORIA
RC·132

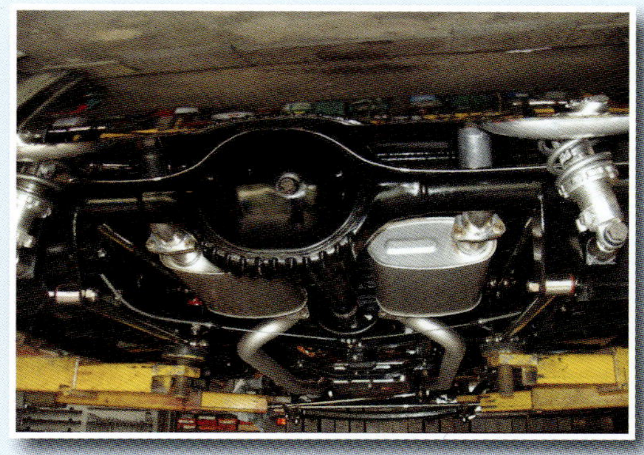

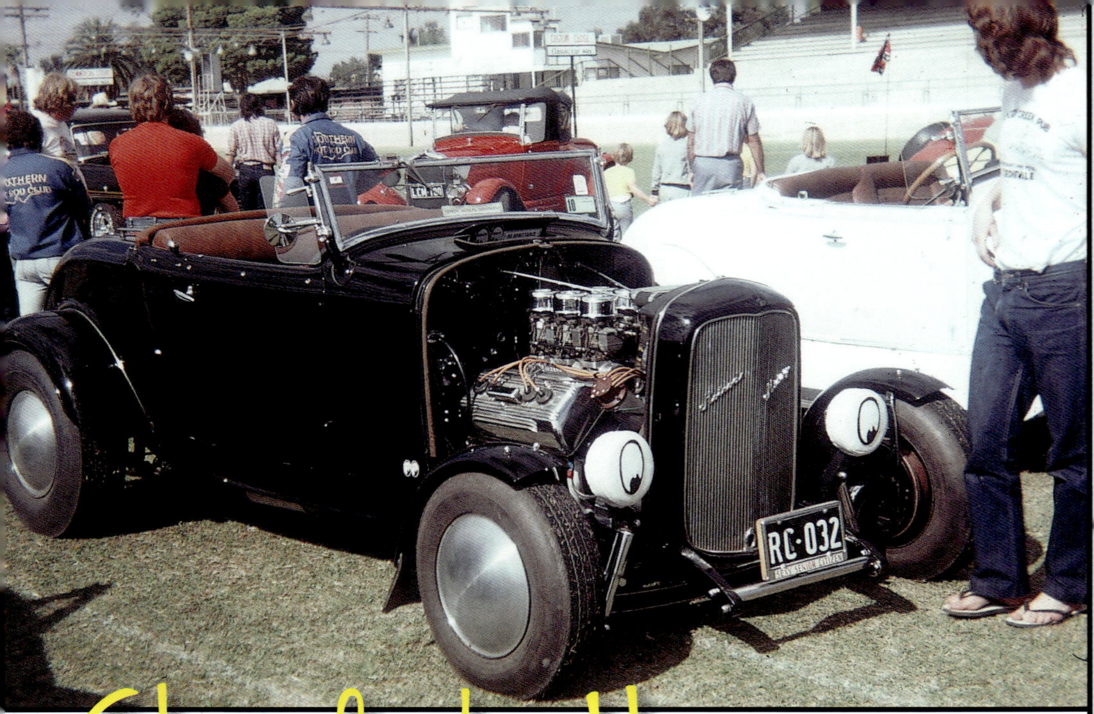

LEFT: Ray purchased this '32 Ford roadster in 1962 and has kept it ever since. Over the years it has had several different running gear combinations but none more special than the genuine Ardun headed flathead that it has in these pictures. The roadster is shown in this photo at the Mildura Street Rod Nationals in 1983 when it ran steel wheels with full Moon discs and quaint Mooneyes headlight covers. The engine with Ardun heads was purchased years ago from Mildura rodder Roger Harrison. It is fed by six Stromberg 97 carbies on log manifolds.

Charlie's Heritage

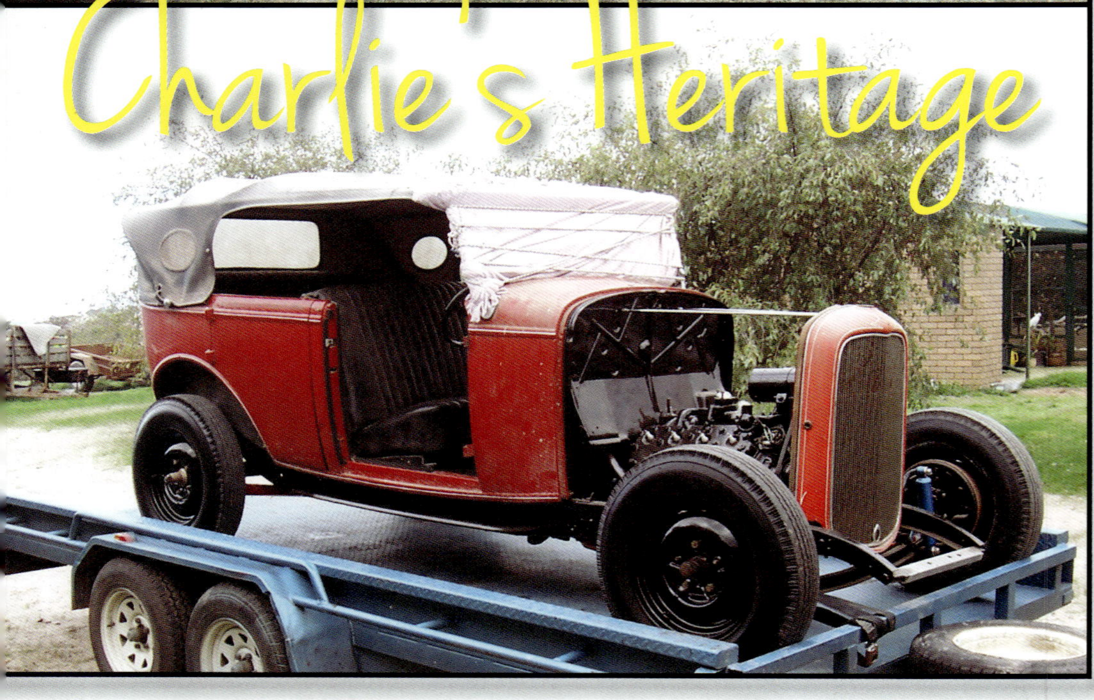

LEFT: Ray's '32 Ford tourer has always been flathead powered and was driven mostly in hiboy form with bobbed rear fenders and cycle front fenders. It is shown here on the day it went to a new owner.

BELOW LEFT: The five window coupe became Ray's main street rod for many years after it hit the road in 1973. This photo was taken at the Narrandera Street Rod Nationals in 1973 when the front fenders were still in primer and the engine bay housed a stock 283 Chevy engine.

BELOW: This photo taken in Canberra in the mid '70s shows the coupe with a full paint job and flames added. Note the Holden front suspension and Tasmanian registration plate that it carried for several years. The rebuild of the coupe to how you now see it in this article started in 2015.

RAY CHARLTON'S LIFE IN HOT RODDING

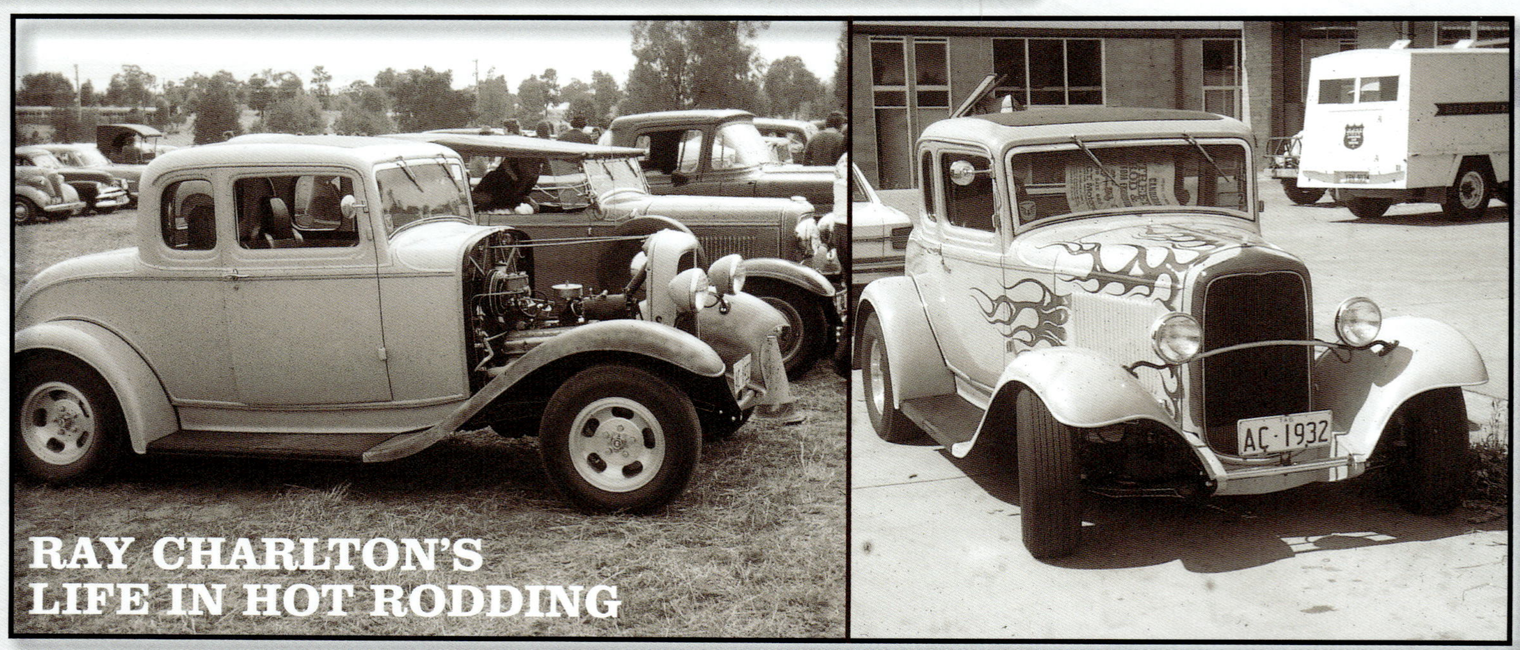

BELOW & LEFT: Ray returned to racing in the late 1990s but this time it was the Lake Gairdner dry lakes racing that distracted him for several years. The red roadster started out as a joint venture with Kevin Parker and it initially ran the Chevy engine out of the black roadster that powered it to a creditable 153 mph. A built 350 followed that, but was destroyed while racing and was replaced with a 372 cubic inch version that was built to the limit for the class and fed by a twin tunnel ram manifold. Consistent results were generally enjoyed with a best speed of 189 mph. but eventually the expense and limited opportunities to race saw the roadster retired. Ray is slowly working toward putting it on the street with flathead running gear that has now been installed.

RIGHT: When racing forays often meant Ray's '34 Chevy Sports Coupe wasn't able to be driven to work the next morning after a meeting he decided a pure race car might be more appropriate. That pure race car took the form of this Model A Ford based altered that ran a modified Holden grey motor and jacked up front end for better weight transfer. The altered was campaigned regularly at Riverside and Ray drove it for the last time at the opening meeting of Calder Dragway after selling it to a new owner.

Euro/UK Nationals

Words & Photos: Larry O'Toole

OLD WARDEN PARK, BIGGLESWADE, BEDFORDSHIRE, ENGLAND

The European Street Rod Nationals is held annually and rotates around the various countries in Europe that have active street rod associations. For 2017 the event was set for the UK so a decision was taken by the NSRA-UK to team it with their own NSRA Hot Rod Supernationals. The Supernationals is held at Shuttleworth House near Old Warden, a grand mansion property that now houses an educational facility along with special attractions such as the Shuttleworth Collection (pre-World War II aeroplanes) and the Swiss Garden.

In effect, the first two days of the combined event was to be the European Nationals, on Wednesday and Thursday (August 9 and 10), followed by the Supernationals on Friday, Saturday and Sunday (August 11, 12 and 13). Heavy rain washed out all activity other than registrations on the Wednesday but it was a much clearer morning on Thursday so entrants were soon lining up for the day's activity, a cruise via a series of scenic backroads to the

Sharnbrook Hotel where there was a smorgasbord lunch, followed by a Blues Brothers show in a section of the show and shine area.

Later in the afternoon the entrants made their way back to Old Warden for the beginning of the Supernationals. For those with energy left there was a disco in the big marquee in the evening.

Friday dawned bright and sunny and the lines of rods and customs filtered into the venue continuously. There was little organised activity on this day apart from the prize-giving for the Euronats at 12:30pm and some light entertainment in the NSRA Hospitality Tent. There were seven countries represented at the Euronats with cars coming from France, Germany, Belgium, Netherlands, Sweden, Denmark and the United Kingdom.

It was full-on Hot Rod Supernats on Saturday when the venue suddenly filled with entrants' cars and everything was set for a big weekend. The main feature of this day was a cruise to the Milton Keynes Museum some 30 miles from Old Warden. Those

TOP: Flags represent all of the countries that have a street rod association in Europe – plus the USA flag.
ABOVE: Several of the Euro Nats entrants, led by Brian Watson's '33 Ford coupe, line up in the display area early on the Thursday when the rain went away.
ABOVE RIGHT: Flamed '32 Ford hiboy roadster is an outstanding rod owned by Kevin Foster.
RIGHT: The superbly finished '50 Mercury lead sled of Teri Smith.

TOP LEFT: Chopped and dropped, bright red Pop van is a tough looking customer with blown V8 powerplant.
TOP RIGHT: At the opposite end of the scale is this neat little '37 Fiat Topolino of Jacqui Kowalewsky.
INSET ABOVE LEFT: Andrew Chaddock made this incredible mini VW Kombi as his camper to tow behind his immaculate Pop.
MAIN PIC: Entrants had their picture taken with a bi-plane as they were leaving for the cruise to the Sharnbrook Hotel. Geoff Cave owns the '35 Ford coupe.
ABOVE LEFT: From Germany was this tidy '38 Ford coupe in two tone green owned by Dieter Anthofer.
ABOVE: Graham Slater's swoopy custom is late model Jaguar based and reminiscent of Australia's "Effijy".
LEFT: A pair of '32 Ford roadsters head this line up of mostly European visitors.

LEFT: Very few of these remain, even in the UK. It's a Morris Z van owned by Reuben Harris and finished in two tone bronze paintwork.

BELOW: Equal to any '34 Ford hiboy from anywhere else in the world is this yellow, chopped example owned by Kevin Foster.

BELOW CLOCKWISE: Nose to nose '32 Fords makes an interesting comparison. The orange modified of John Proctor and Bill O'Connell is Model A based but uses a Pop chassis and running gear. Latest Hall of Famers inductees Mike and June Key's '32 Ford three window coupe is a superb piece. Parked alongside is Tim Hammond's hand crafted '32 roadster. Two tone '28 Model A Tudor has spoke front wheels, a top chop and custom made splash apron.

that went enjoyed the pleasant cruise through the countryside. Back at Old Warden various forms of entertainment were on offer from movies for the kids to live bands and the impressive "Circle of Death" vintage stunt motorcycle show.

The weather was perfect for the final day of the Supernats and the fans rolled in non-stop from the minute the public gates opened. Likewise for entrants with many day-trippers swelling the car numbers beyond capacity so an overflow area was opened up behind the trade stands. There was plenty to do and see with trade stands surrounding the large show field, the Wall of Death motorcycle stunt show running all day and over 1500 pre-'72 cars to check out at close quarters. The variety of cars on show was fantastic with everything from classic American cars to locally bred English tin and even a few Aussie utes.

Presentations started late in the afternoon and when it finally got down to the Top Ten and the Entrants Choice for Top Car, all of the winners proved to be popular choices.

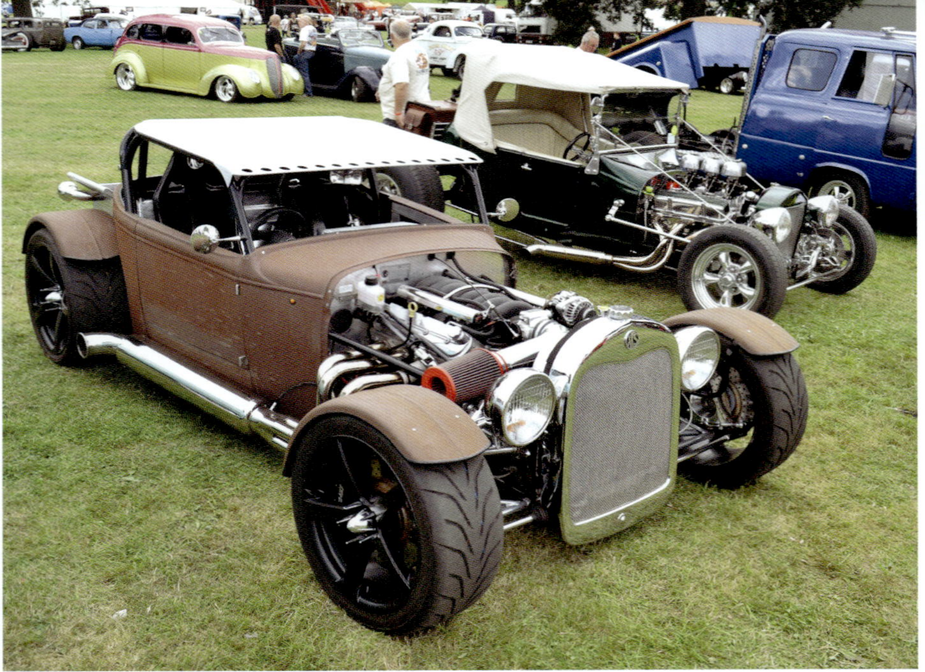

ABOVE: A different approach to building a Model A hot rod is displayed in this low-slung bucket style, independent suspended rocket that looks like it could mix it with sports car racers on the track.

TOP LEFT: Ground hugging two door 100E Pop is typical of the high standard, locally inspired customs now stamping their mark on the hobby in no uncertain terms.

ABOVE LEFT: Candy red and chopped '50 Chevy pickup was a Top Ten finalist for owner Clive Hardy.

LEFT: Gasser style '57 Chevy looks to be an actual US drag strip refugee transplanted to the UK by owner Simon Devos. It is powered by a 460 Ford V8 with a 12 bolt Chevy rear end.

BELOW LEFT: Mini rods are always popular at the Supernationals and Anwar Felicien-Springall's Fordson delivery van was a trophy winner at presentations time for Best Tot Rod.

BELOW: There's a full feature on Andy Saunders incredible Cord custom elsewhere in this issue. It was built from a wasted original Cord and features a hand formed body.

MAIN: A large group of the '34 Fords in attendance at the Hot Rod Supernationals gathered for a group photo.

TOP LEFT: Graphic photo shows just how low this Model A coupe sits when the air-bags are deflated.
TOP RIGHT & INSET: Exhibiting elements of steam punk design is Johnny Morris''48 Ford F-1 truck with trunks for tool boxes, Cummins 6BT turbo diesel with intercooler, five speed ZF gearbox, air-bag suspension all round and hydraulic tipping tray.

FAR LEFT: Two Door MkI Cortina is a brilliant example of the breed minus bumpers and plus candy paint.

LEFT: Ditto this petite but tough Anglia notch-back two door that is fully equipped for drag racing.

BELOW: American guest Voodoo Larry laid some stripes on the trunk lid of this fastback Chevy in front of an appreciative audience.

ABOVE: Morris Minor ute was one of several Aussie utes entered at the Supernationals. The tidy red runner had louvred engine hood, widened steel wheels and tons of appeal.

ABOVE: Don't pick a fight with this one. Diminutive Pop two door owned by Danny Wilson has big block Chev running gear, trick body work with raised rear wheel arches and a brillant flame job over glossy black paint.

ABOVE: Everyone agreed that Steven Roberts' V6 Mondeo powered '59 Thames van was outstanding, voting it the Participants Choice winner of the Supernationals.
ABOVE RIGHT: Another outstanding trophy winner was the '59 Chevy Apache pickup of young rodder Wade Nortcliff.
RIGHT: Lop the top off a '48 Austin Dorset and smooth up the rest of the body and you have an outstanding custom owned by John Stearman.
BELOW RIGHT: Custom made two door body conversion on this MkI Consul looks like it came from the factory that way.

ABOVE: Blown small block Chevy power in this grey Pop two door sedan would make for an exciting ride at full tilt.

ABOVE LEFT: Orange full-fendered and rodded Y Model Ford two door sedan featured DOHC four cylinder engine, Vauxhall Viva front end and Center Lines.
ABOVE: Chopped and dropped VW beetle looks nasty with skinny wheels and exposed flat four engine.
BELOW: At first glance you could mistake this scaled down pickup for a full size version but it's little bigger than a mini-rod.

ABOVE: Another Y Model Ford, this time a fenderless version owned by John Proctor and stuffed full of blown Daimler Hemi engine.

RIGHT: These Tot Rod owners get to watch the kids drive-in movies in style.

BELOW: Dune buggies seem to be making a come-back all around the world. This trio sparkles in the sunshine while their owners check out all of the other cars at the Supernationals.

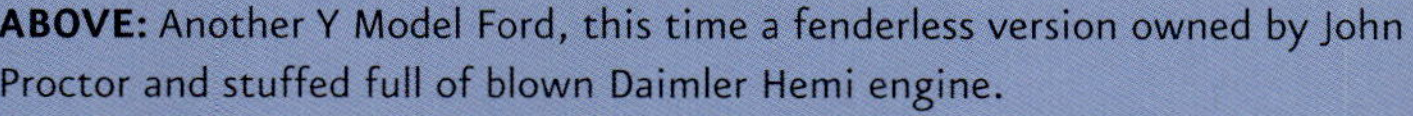

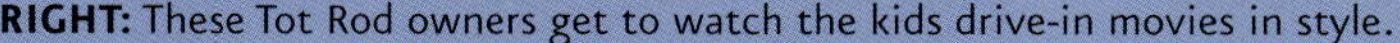

ABOVE: The clean lines of Brian Watson's 33 Ford hiboy coupe make it a stand out rod.

ABOVE LEFT: What looks like a Ford Pop pickup actually has what appears to be a Morris based cab section with Pop front sheet metal and custom bed.

ABOVE: Two tone and flamed '39 Chevy coupe has custom made grille and chrome billet wheels.

BELOW: The Squire Wagon version of the 100E Anglia is one of the rarer body styles, making Lisa and Warren Breslin's blue '58 example even more desirable.

LEFT: No matter how young you can still have fun at the Supernationals, especially when you have a cool set of wheels like this custom Radio Flyer wagon.

ABOVE: Russell Doyle's mild custom '56 Studebaker pickup has centrally mounted bullet in the grille and dechromed body for a smooth overall style.

RIGHT: Vintage "Houndog 1" slingshot dragster from 1962 owned by Nobby Hills has blown Jaguar six cylinder engine.

MAIN PIC: An impromptu show and shine took place in the parking lot at the Milton Keynes Museum, the destination for Saturday's cruise.

RIGHT: Jacked up Austin gasser looks the part but has street tyres fitted for practical everyday driving.

ABOVE: Stock bodied Pop van looks smooth in straight grey paint with 3.9 V6 engine and Weld wheels.

ABOVE RIGHT: The best jalopy tradition is exemplified in this fenderless Model A roadster pickup.

MAIN: All of the trophy winners from the Supernationals lined up in front of Shuttleworth House for a photo session to conclude the event. The Shuttleworth House property is now an agricultural college with private air museum and landing strip attached.

BELOW: Smooth looking mild custom sedan is so well done it gives away no clue to its original identity. Elements of the body look Chevy related, as does the front bumper but there is little else that can be readily recognised.

BELOW RIGHT: Mick Harle owns the slick Ford pickup that features '35 engine hood but '36 grille. Painted bent spoke wires set the grey metallic paint off perfectly.

RIGHT: Low riding, channelled '32 Ford roadster is Ricky Stapleton's period perfect hot rod that use split 'bones and a split windscreen.

BELOW: Mild custom MkII Consul has been beautifully executed. Changes include conversion to two door, pillarless configuration and slanted taillights.

BELOW RIGHT: Another customised English Ford, this time a MkII Zephyr built by Kevin Smith that has been converted to two door, fitted with Buick inspired custom grille and quad headlights. The low turret profile suggests it was originally a '60 model.

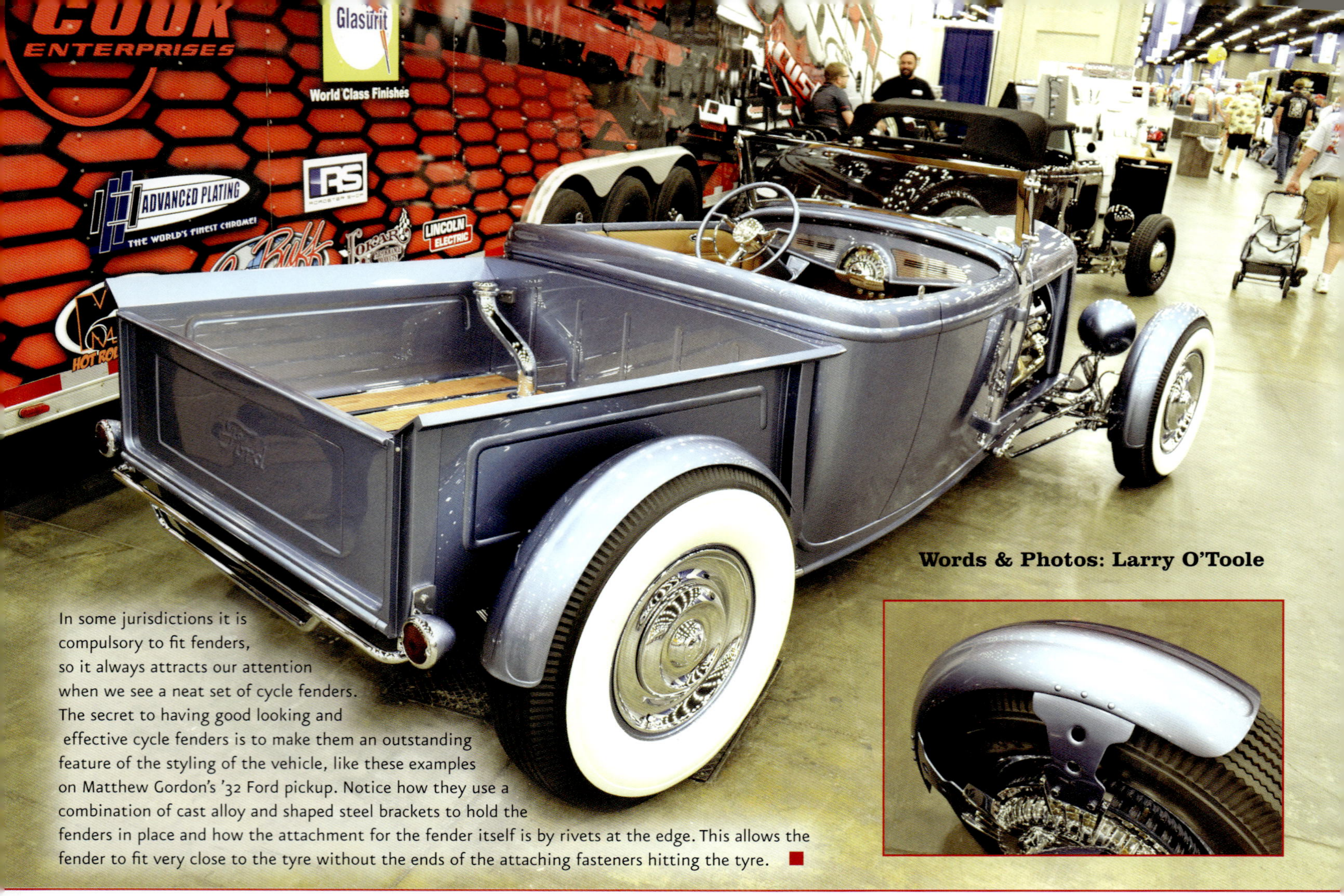

In some jurisdictions it is compulsory to fit fenders, so it always attracts our attention when we see a neat set of cycle fenders. The secret to having good looking and effective cycle fenders is to make them an outstanding feature of the styling of the vehicle, like these examples on Matthew Gordon's '32 Ford pickup. Notice how they use a combination of cast alloy and shaped steel brackets to hold the fenders in place and how the attachment for the fender itself is by rivets at the edge. This allows the fender to fit very close to the tyre without the ends of the attaching fasteners hitting the tyre. ■

Words & Photos: Larry O'Toole

HOT RODDERS' *Handy hints*

Resourceful hot rodders are always coming up with neat ideas to do things differently. That's what this article is about, how to be resourceful with your individual ideas as these clever rodders have been.

Don't worry if you're not one for readily coming up with unique concepts, feed your mind with these examples and then adapt and use them to suit your own purposes. You might even find your mental strengths enhanced to such an extent that you soon come up with your own unique ideas that become the subject of future Rodding Hints articles.

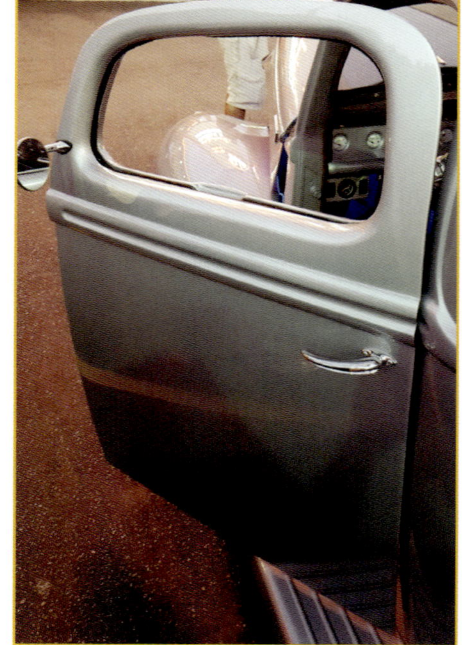

LEFT: The popularity of bomber style seats has caused legal complications in some instances where the regulations call for seats to have a padded or upholstered surface. Here's a pair of such seats that do meet the requirements by having custom made and trimmed inserts that fit into the shape of the polished alloy bomber seats. You can have your cake and eat it!

ABOVE RIGHT: It's not uncommon to convert early vehicles to suicide door opening but it is to find the original exterior handle still in place at the rear edge of the door. The owner of this '40 Ford pickup even managed to make this change but still have the handle operate the door latch at the leading edge of the door.

ABOVE: This orange Track style roadster is an interesting combination of parts. The chassis and running gear is Ford Anglia or Popular but the body is Model A with '32 Ford grille. It's a style you can love or hate but you must admit the windscreen mounting is clever. The windscreen frame and glass appear to be from a late '30s car and it is very simply bolted in place on the Model A cowl using a simple bracket to hold it to the original Model A windscreen post bases. It is consequently a very easy swap to change to a different style windscreen mounted in a similar fashion, or to bolt and original Model A item back in place.

If you don't like obtrusive exterior mirrors hanging off the side of your early car you might like these simple but very small items made from a cleverly shaped flat steel bracket and using the parabolic insert mirror as used as an addition to larger towing mirrors.

Here's another Model A Ford based rod that is quite literally loaded with clever ideas. The vehicle is mounted to a custom made tubular frame that incorporates a full roll cage and independent suspension at front and rear. Everywhere you look there are custom made brackets like the rear fender mounts and taillight mounts, the interior has race inspired alloy panels and typical race car bucket seats. The use of a Model A grille shell and headlights keeps the early style accents intact while the roofed roll cage is simple and clever. LS Chevy running gear ensures this would be a very fast car that is built to handle well when driven hard. It's an overall package that looks the part and has that chunky hunkered down style accentuated by the bulky side exhaust pipes and wide racing tyres. Bet it is fun to drive!

ABOVE: Loads more clever ideas on a Ford Popular from the UK that has custom made grille inserts bars mounted behind the openings in the grille and hood sides. The whole front tilts forward for access to the engine and uses chrome plated covered locks to hold it in place, similar to those used for doors or trunks on older vehicles. Small round lights have been added to the lower front fenders as turn signals.

LEFT & ABOVE: There's that clever original door handle still in place at the rear edge of the door again on this Popular and the owner has made a short prop that fits to the suicide opening door latch to hold the door open when the vehicle is on display. Go the rear and we find a trunk lid converted to side opening style with burst-proof latch and gas ram to hold it open. Next check out the engine bay where we find a small block Ford V8 engine replacing the tiny original four cylinder engine, thanks to a hefty firewall set-back. Notice how the area surrounding the firewall has strong square structures that retain and increase the body strength in this vital area and provide a substantial mounting point for the radiator strut rod.

Lots of subtle changes here on a Model A roadster. Rear fenders have been shortened, the lower rear panel has been lengthened and blended into the lower panel and the slotted tail light openings incorporated at each corner. Look closely and you will also see a subtle bulge in the centre of the boot lid so you can get your fingers under it to lift the lid. Finally we have neat rounded cut-outs in the lower panel to accommodate the exhaust tailpipes and a recess for the registration plate. Neat work!

The same blue Model A has windshield posts blended into the cowl and painted the same as the body and the painted running boards have simple chromed protection strips added to the top for a nice highlight.

This is one of the smartest ideas I have seen in a long while. The owner of this English Ford Popular has completely redesigned the car to use V8 running gear and consequently it has much wider wheels, particularly on the rear – yet they look like stock original Popular wheels! Close inspection (and it really does have to be close) reveal that the car is fitted with older style Center Line wheels that have covers made from what look like the original Popular wheels. This conversion was so well executed it was impossible to tell if the covers were actually Popular wheels cut down so they could be used as a cap, or whether they were made from fibreglass replicas of original wheels that were then painted to match the body.

Attention to detail is foremost in this picture. The owner of the Model A pickup, Adam Endicott has gone to great lengths to have the folks at Star Kustom Shop of Riverside, California inset the doors into the body. Originally they overlapped the door opening so this is not an easy or straightforward task, especially as the cabin has also been stretched five inches by adding to the width of the doors and the section of cabin immediately to the rear of the doors. The body has also been subtly channelled over the Deuce chassis by 1-1/2 inches. Drip rails above the doors have been eliminated and if you look closely at the leading edge of the pickup bed you will notice that it has also been reshaped to follow the curve of the cabin. Finally the lower edge of the bed has been reworked with a new integrated cover that cleans up the lines and added louvres give it a "hot rod" style.

LEFT: Original style rubber covered running boards on '30s era street rods have been making a comeback, but this example is a little different. Instead of completely covering the running board with the rubber as is done originally Jon Wright has opted for an inset style rubber pad that gives his '36 roadster a touch of individual class.

ABOVE: The black paint on Jon Wright's custom '36 Ford roadster is so deep it makes it a little difficult to see the changes made here easily. A vaguely '37 Ford style headlight has been blended into the '36 front fender with a slightly raised edge around the opening and a subtle peak at the top. The headlight uses a conventional sealed beam headlight insert but the tiny turn signal stands alone underneath it. You might think that turn signal light is too small to be effective, but these days you can purchase extremely bright LED lights for this purpose that, despite their size, emit a very bright light that other drivers can't miss. Also note the custom grille insert and the use of a ribbed DeSoto style bumper with neatly fitted filler tray in the space between bumper and fender.

Campers don't come much more unique than this tidy example that is towed behind Andrew Chaddock's dark blue Ford Popular in the UK. The camper is made from sections of VW Kombi van but is much smaller than the original Kombi. A pop-top allows the occupant to stand up inside the camper and it is fitted with most amenities needed for comfortable accommodation while at the rod runs. Clever badges declaring it a "Crampervan" and the "Should Have Gone to Spec Savers" quote bring a smile to casual observers.

Another simple idea added to a Ford Popular in the UK is this simple exterior mirror mount that is bolted to the door hinge instead of through the sheet metal of the door itself. Mounted in this position it will be much less subject to vibration and there's no need for another hole in the door skin.

On the same car is this matching design side marker light that has been mounted into the forward corner of the hood side panel. Obviously pirated off a later model car it looks like it belongs here and would be visible from the front and side when in operation.

This black T bucket has lots of custom touches including the cast alloy taillight and turn signal covers. Versions of these could be used over a simple and cheap accessory taillight for an individual custom effect as seen here.
The same T bucket has another clever item in its folding top release. The top is too low for the driver and passenger to slide in through the side of the vehicle but pull the trigger on the mechanism inside and the whole top section pivots upward and back for easy entry or egress.
It can be hard to make an alternator look tidy on an exposed engine but this simple cover does the trick on Allen White's T bucket. The holes allow ventilation and a slot accommodates the adjustment slide and a coat of hammer tone paint lets it blend into its surrounds.

There are so many clever changes to Steven Roberts' Popular van it would be hard to list them all. Here are some of the most obvious ones. The engine hood has been lengthened and the front bumper made into bumperettes that conform to the shape of the grille panel. Doors have been lengthened and wheel arch openings reworked into a more pleasing shape. Virtually every exterior panel has been changed in some way. The rear doors have been changed to an upper and lower tailgate and the rear windows made larger but retain their original shape.

www.graffitipub.com.au

How clean are the body liners on this '28 Model A Ford? The engine hood has been converted to three piece but doesn't have any external means of holding it shut. Stainless steel bolts fitted to where the original clamps fitted now only retain the hood shelves that are perfectly fitted where they meet the front fender and valance panel. Viewed from the other side we can see that the side panels are actually secured from inside the engine bay and the release is a rod that slides back and forth from the passenger compartment to engage in small brackets that extend from the top piece into the lower panel. All very neat and tidy.

Clean and simple always looks good as shown by this rear end shot of Ken Matthews' Model A Sport Coupe, the same car as shown at left. The taillights are stock repro Model A items but they have been mounted directly to the fender, eliminating the normal mounting stem. The registration plate is bolted to the car so that there is a small space between it and the body and the chrome cylindrical shaped retaining bolts have the illuminating lights hidden inside them.

Also from Ken Matthews' coupe we have a set of windshield wipers that mount through the header panel where they are hidden by the sunshade. The blades are angled so that when parked they sit horizontally across the top of the windshield frame where they are hardly noticed. Inside the mechanism is hidden behind a trimmed header panel with a shaped vinyl cover over the wiper motor itself.

No need to pay top dollar for a specially cast triple carburettor manifold when you can achieve the same effect like Brian Carvolth did with this triple adaptor. The cast aluminium adaptor bolts to a normal four barrel carburettor manifold and in turn takes the triple two barrels on top. The benefit is you don't need to use (or tune) the triple carbs if you don't want to, just run off the centre two barrel for economy and looks. Alternatively you can do as Brian has and use a progressive linkage to run on the centre carb for regular use but floor the throttle and you get all three. The adaptor is a commercial piece from Vintage Speed.

One of my favourite subjects at shows is the retaining fences used to separate your pride and joy from the viewing public. Over many years of visiting and photographing shows I have seen many displays spoilt by a poor choice when it comes to this barrier. In short, the less intrusive the fence, the better, particularly if you are photographer. A beautiful car is very hard to photograph if it is surrounded by a too high fence, even more so if it is white or a bright coloured rope. On these two pages are several examples of very good show barriers because they serve their purpose well but don't restrict your view of the vehicle. At top left wooden planks have been used to contruct long boxes that hide all the wiring for the spotlights that are mounted into the corners of the barrier. Floor covering is a complimentary piece of flooring vinyl for a clean effect. Short stands under each wheel lift the vehicle up slightly to a better viewing height. Above right is the same idea made from polished tubing with clear acetate supports holding the two sections of tubing apart. Once again the wiring for the mounted spotlights is hidden inside the tubing and there's a clean piece of contrasting carpet under the raised car. Below is an even simpler barrier made from exhaust tubing with bolt together flanges making assembly and transport easy. Hammer tone paint on the barrier is complimentary to the colour of the chassis making it all look like it belongs together. Bottom right is again exhaust tubing but this time laid straight onto the carpet on the floor. All you need is a barrier that subtly says, "Stay on that side". At bottom left there is no barrier at all, just plastic interlocking floor tiles with a tapered outer trim that delineates the vehicle stand. Even though there is no barrier as such, show patrons usually respect the space.

On this page we have a few more variations on the same theme. Above and below short wooden posts have been used as the supports for polished tube rails that are shin high. The lower example also has the spotlight mounts fitted to the bottom wooden rail with wiring hidden underneath. Wheel stands on one side only allow the vehicle to be tilted for better viewing of the detailed underside that is further enhanced by large mirrors on the floor. The low fence at right is similar to those shown on the left page but this one is made from painted pvc plumbing pipe. The motorcycle owner at lower right has used part of his themed display as the barrier in the form of sand bags loosely stacked around the perimeter.

Deuce hiboys can look a little "gappy" at the rear when the frame horn covers are left off as they tend to only look right when the vehicle is fully fendered. Gary Brown's hiboy looks neater because the lower end of the quarter panels have been extended to wrap around the ends of the fuel tank and fill this area where the frame horn covers normally fit. Also check out the neat registration plate recess that has been subtly let into the rear panel and then outlined with a chrome trim.

There are amazing details all over Rick Werner's '32 Ford pickup but in this view you can readily appreciate the superb workmanship in the radiator shroud that is painted and detailed to the same standard as the rest of the vehicle. That way it becomes its own highlight, rather than an "added on" piece. Also note the neatly fitted and polished exhaust cover that is required in many jurisdictions when the exhaust header extends outside the engine bay.

On early Model A roadster pickups the door usually overlaps the surrounding bodywork but on this example it has been modified to fit flush. This particular vehicle has also been fitted with burst-proof door latches that prevent the door "bouncing" in its opening and the owner has incorporated a neat little push button release in the top edge of the door where it serves as both inner and outer door release.

Want to play in the modified car playgound but don't have any budget to work with? Why not do as this owner has and start with a vehicle you can afford, in this case a '65 Falcon Fairmont wagon and keep the appointments low budget to suit? Cleanly detailed wheel caps from a later model Falcon, satin vinyl wrap with side scallop and original accessories like the venetion blinds and the sun visor and you are in the game. Finish off the effect with some neat graphics on the sun visor and the job is complete.

Get the feeling there is something missing from this early Falcon engine bay? Yes, the inner suspension towers have gone, greatly enhancing the amount of engine space available and making access around it very easy. In this case the front suspension has been replaced completely with a bolt-in unit from a Mitsubishi L300 and its towers fit inside the fender well.

The rear end of the same vehicle shows another clever idea in the form of abbreviated chromed bumperettes. These are normally rubber items that wrap around the corners of the quarter panels but they are always damaged on original vehicles. Rather than just replace them this owner has made his own from large diameter exhaust tubing and then had them chromed.

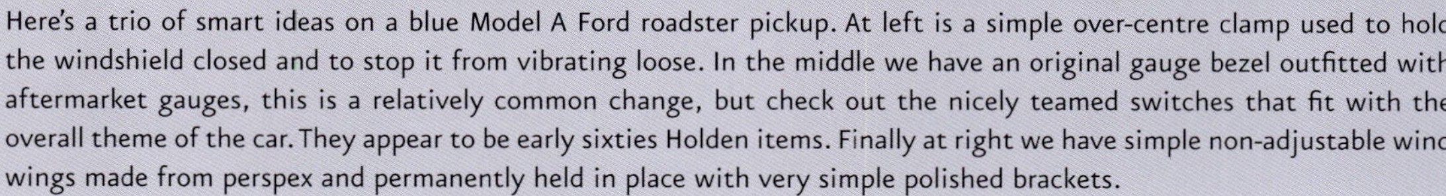

Here's a trio of smart ideas on a blue Model A Ford roadster pickup. At left is a simple over-centre clamp used to hold the windshield closed and to stop it from vibrating loose. In the middle we have an original gauge bezel outfitted with aftermarket gauges, this is a relatively common change, but check out the nicely teamed switches that fit with the overall theme of the car. They appear to be early sixties Holden items. Finally at right we have simple non-adjustable wind wings made from perspex and permanently held in place with very simple polished brackets.

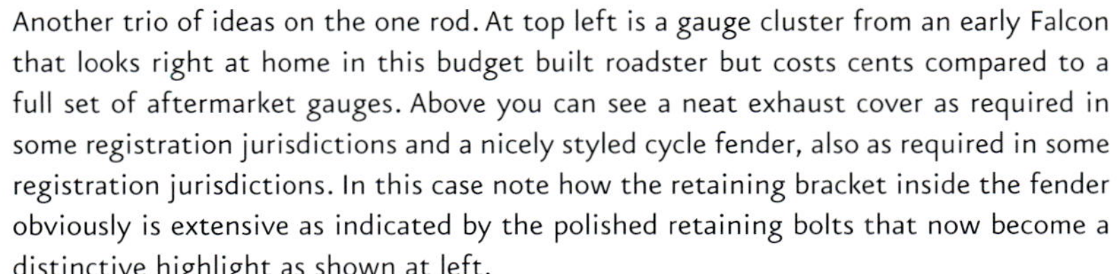

Another trio of ideas on the one rod. At top left is a gauge cluster from an early Falcon that looks right at home in this budget built roadster but costs cents compared to a full set of aftermarket gauges. Above you can see a neat exhaust cover as required in some registration jurisdictions and a nicely styled cycle fender, also as required in some registration jurisdictions. In this case note how the retaining bracket inside the fender obviously is extensive as indicated by the polished retaining bolts that now become a distinctive highlight as shown at left.

It is relatively common to fit burst-proof door latches to early doors on a street rod but look how Mark Harris mounted his above the belt line of the door and hooked them to original style outer door handles that are glossy black instead of chromed, in keeping with the same theme throughout the '40 Chevy truck.

It's not often you see contrasting styling elements teamed together so well as we see on this Chevy pickup. It combines the latest large diameter aftermarket wheels with very low profile tyres and a paint scheme more reminiscent of having been dragged out of a barn, yet given a suave satin clear finish that adds a classy feel to the truck. Air-bag suspension allows it to sit on the deck.

The engine bay reveals more contrasting style elements with a V8 engine that has been painted and detailed to look as if it is brand new from the factory. The white firewall and inner fenders add to the spectacle by isolating the engine in its own space and concentrating the viewer's gaze immediately on the engine. When it all looks this clean and tidy, who needs chrome dress-up?

The Boogaloo Invitational proved to be a popular event when it was first staged in 2016. It's only natural that a first time event would achieve a good measure of support, but would it transfer into the second year? That question was answered with a resounding yes when Boogaloo #2 opened at the Wattle Flat Reserve in Castlemaine on Friday April 28, 2017.

Action was subdued on the first overcast but fine day as many were still at work, or making their way to Castlemaine, but when the gates opened on Saturday morning period style hot rods, customs, plus chopper and bobber bikes from all over Australia streamed into the venue. Misty rain was barely heavy enough to cause any concern and cleared as the morning progressed. Bikes assembled at the front of the display area and cars to the rear, flanked down both sides by a suitable array of trade stands and headed by the bar and food vendors at the point of the triangular shaped area.

When you see over 300 rods and bikes of similar style all assembled together it certainly creates a unique atmosphere and one that everyone present appreciated. Instead of live bands playing throughout the day, the appropriate background music was supplied by a DJ. Right through the day there was a constant flow of general public pouring in for a look at the fantastic display of nostalgic cars and bikes, so much so that there was a sea of people mixed in with the cars all the time. It all made for a happy relaxed time for everyone.

After the sun went down screenings of short hot rod and chopper themed films by local and international film makers were shown on the big screen followed by DJs playing a wide variety of tunes to entertain the mostly younger crowd. All this was a refreshing change to the rock and roll and rockabilly music usually found at hot rod events. A delicious range of kustom cocktails and craft beers flowed over the bar, fire pits provided some much needed warmth and a party atmosphere with a care-free and unpretentious attitude ensured everyone was having a great time. Food vendors stayed open 'til late and the campgrounds were abuzz with folks enjoying good times until well into the night.

Sunday morning dawned to the wispy smoke of dying campfires and a troubling problem for entrants who stayed on site. The portable toilets brought in for the event were unable to cope with the size of the large Saturday crowd and Saturday night revellers and were all in dire need of servicing by a mobile septic truck. One did arrive to take care of the problem but many found they couldn't wait and packed up early.

LEFT: Bobber bikes and early style choppers are welcome at The Boogaloo and are displayed together near the front of the Wattle Flat venue in Castlemaine.

MAIN: The grounds didn't open to entrants until mid afternoon on the Friday by which time there was a long line of waiting participants. Mark Bailey is about to enter the gateway in his Model T Ford roadster on '32 rails with Model A grille and flathead running gear. That's the open engine bay of Kerry Brown's '39 Ford in the foreground, housing a triple 97 Stromberg equipped small block Chevy engine. The Boogaloo Invitational 2017 was held on the last weekend of April.

ABOVE: You won't find a smarter Model A pickup than the fenderless, small block Chevy powered '30 model version owned by Adam Pohl.

ABOVE RIGHT: John Lynch owns the beater style '34 Ford three window coupe that features an Ardun equipped flathead in the engine bay.

RIGHT: Low slung and chopped '57 Buick finished in two tone blue and white is a tidy piece. It belongs to Adrian Skirde.

ABOVE: Front and centre is the channelled Model A roadster of Kyle De Kuijer with flathead engine that wears unique marine engine covers. Parking for the many bobber and early style chopper bikes is all together at the front of the display area.

LEFT: Checking in at the gate includes inspection of invite acceptance and the issue of a Boogaloo sticker. Bobber bikes like this green example are a feature of the unique event.

BELOW LEFT: Banger powered Moel A roadster pickup looks fantastic in glossy black with bright red mechanicals and cream wire wheels.

BELOW: Savagely chopped '30 Model A coupe with skinny spindle mount front wheels, Deuce grille and split headlight bar has a style all of its own. It belongs to Ben Love.

ABOVE: What a profile! James Gamble's '56 Mercury sled is chopped and dropped in keeping with the best of the tradition and stops casual viewers in their tracks. It's awesome!

ABOVE: Burgo and Charlie Falzon entertained the crowd by starting up the blown Hemi engine in the '32 Ford pickup from time to time.
ABOVE RIGHT: How about an FJ Holden with Norman supercharged grey motor? Grantley Strapps brought it along to the delight of the big crowd.
RIGHT: Fitting the invite criteria perfectly is this dark brown '30 Model A Ford hiboy roadster with '35 wire wheels, flathead running gear and neatly fitted cycle fenders. Owner is Scott Montgomery.

ABOVE: Wire wheeled '35 Ford five window coupe has blown flathead power topped with a trio of Stromberg 97 carbies.
RIGHT: Radically chopped '48 Ford coupe has shadow panels over bare metal for a striking effect. Owner Mark Apap went home with the Smiths Kustoms' King Kustom trophy.

The Boogaloo Invitational

ABOVE: Kathleen Aldrick's '35 Ford Tudor provides space for all the family to ride along.

ABOVE LEFT: Chris Wells owns this tidy chopped and channelled '30 Model A coupe with 331 Hemi engine and '36 Ford dash.

LEFT: Back in the sixties this little Model A pickup was a competitor at the Riverside Drags in Melbourne. These days it lives in Neal Canan's shed.

ABOVE: Caddy wheel caps grace the wheels of this '51 Chevy pickup that has many subtle custom touches.

LEFT: One of the originals is Peter Swift's black '24 bucket that was built in 1962 and remains essentially unchanged to this day.

ABOVE: Kyle Smith's radically chopped and channelled, blown small block Chevy powered Model A Tudor is flanked by a pair of pickups.
BELOW: Sometimes waiting to get in can test the patience of the best of cooling systems. It all becomes part of the fun around the campfire later.

BELOW: Chris Wells' Model A coupe that travelled down from the Sunshine Coast in Queensland took home the Kardinals Club Pick award.
BOTTOM: Like something from a farm yard scene in the 1930s, this pair of old Fords await the return of their owners. Model T at left, Model A at right.

www.graffitipub.com.au

ABOVE: Loaded up with all of the camping gear, Ben Love's '58 Chevy pickup rolls through the entry gate for a weekend of fun.
BELOW: Any vantage point will do to get the "right" picture.

ABOVE: Travis Constantine's early Model A coupe retains the original four banger engine with quad carbs, but relies on later '35 Ford wire wheels.
BELOW: James Chisholm's chopped '54 Chev rides low on air-bag suspension.

ABOVE RIGHT: Panel painted Chevy pickup truck is transport for Jordan Kuchel from South Australia.
ABOVE: Custom coupes stick together. On the left is Bob Maloney's '40 Chrysler with Packard grille beside the bare metal '41 Chevy of Kira Jurado.

LEFT: Side on aspect gives the casual onlooker a clear view of the brilliant work of Kyle Smith's super low '30 Model A Ford Tudor with blown small block Chevy engine.

BELOW LEFT: Black and white coupe is a '53 Buick with Caddy caps and ground hugging stance. It belongs to Wazza "Voodoo Daddy" Schwidlewski.

BELOW: Once owned by Old Crow Speed Shop in the USA this hiboy Model A roadster now belongs to Ross Naumov. Flathead Ford enigne is an 8BA version under the alloy hood.

BOTTOM: Line of highly detailed rods from the Spades shows your old hot rod doesn't have to be rusty to fit the entry criteria.

ABOVE: Powder blue '32 Ford pickup with full wheel caps provides perfect rod run transport.
LEFT: Got a bike and an El Camino? Why not bring them both to The Boogaloo and travel in real style?

ABOVE: Gold highlight panels over a white pearl background are perfect for Matt Egan's radically chopped Ford Customline.
ABOVE RIGHT: Side profile of Chris Wells' channelled Model A coupe shows the multi-carbed Chrysler Hemi engine to clear advantage.
RIGHT: The El Diablos Best Kustom award went to this superb black '46 Chevy coupe. It belongs to Manny Marko from the Wise Guys Car Club.
BELOW: Nev Sunderland used his old vintage dragster with injected flathead power for some authentic start ups to the delight of the large crowd.

LEFT: Des Russell and Tesha Mahoney are the folks behind The Boogaloo. The amount of work they put into planning and conducting the event, along with a small band of family and friends, is legendary.
LEFT & BELOW: Des and Tesh's "company cars" are Des' '28 Model A Ford roadster with multi-carbed Oldsmobile Rocket engine and Tesh's '55 Buick (now sold) that has been partly dechromed and radically lowered.

The Boogaloosters

PROFILE: Des Russell & Tesha Mahoney